A Study of the Relationship Between School Culture and Standardized Test Scores

Andrew Lee Smith

DISSERTATION.COM

Boca Raton

A Study of the Relationship Between School Culture and Standardized Test Scores

Dissertation.com
Boca Raton, Florida
USA • 2008

ISBN-10: 1-59942-673-0
ISBN-13: 978-1-59942-673-0

A STUDY OF THE RELATIONSHIP BETWEEN SCHOOL CULTURE AND

STANDARDIZED TEST SCORES

by

Andrew Lee Smith

A Dissertation Presented in Partial Fulfillment

of the Requirements for the Degree

Doctor of Management in Organizational Leadership

University of Phoenix

April 2006

ABSTRACT

The purpose of this quantitative study was to discover the perceptions of school culture and correlate those perceptions with standardized test scores in elementary and secondary schools in southwestern Arizona. The intention of this study was to contribute to the field of education leadership related to student achievement and factors contributing to student achievement including organizational culture. A survey of teachers and administrators in participating schools in southwestern Arizona was completed and correlated with existing student achievement data for those participating schools. The School Culture Survey by Leithwood, Aitken, and Jantzi (2001) was used for the survey instrument, and the Stanford Achievement Test, Ninth Edition, was used to measure student achievement. The survey results and student achievement data were correlated and revealed that a relationship does exist between perceptions of school culture and student achievement.

ACKNOWLEDGMENTS

To my wife, Lisa. To my dad, family, and friends. To all of those who have given me influence and inspiration. Thank you to all the schools, administrators, and teachers who helped me to complete this study. Thank you, Dr. Alex Nagurney, for your assistance and encouragement, and Dr. Kolberg for the reassurance and support to complete this project. Thanks to Dr. Nanna for his wisdom and to Dr. Edwards for the extra push when I really needed one.

TABLE OF CONTENTS

LIST OF TABLES

LIST OF FIGURES

CHAPTER 1: INTRODUCTION

Rollins and Roberts (1998) noted, "Empirical evidence indicates that organizational culture is an important driver of organizational performance" (p. 1). Stolp and Smith (1995) explained that school culture has a powerful influence in schools because it defines the important elements of that school, and the manner in which school community members operate. School leaders with an understanding of culture are aware that teachers and related school personnel commit personal energy to only what they believe and feel is personally important (Deal & Peterson, 1999a). Schools retaining a culture of excellence and high performance inspire the constituency, paralleling the concept that a culture of incompetence perpetuates opposite results. Interest in school culture has gained momentum with the results of research concluding that the culture of a business organization influences the success or lack of success within an organization (Deal & Peterson, 1999a). These results conclude that the same cultural dimensions accounting for increased measurable performance in business may result in increased measurable achievement in schools (Deal & Peterson, 1999a).

Legislation and policies handed down from both federal and state government agencies increase the pressure for schools to perform and measure success similar to a business model. Expectations exist in the form of achievement on standardized tests (Boyles, 2000; Senge et al., 2000). The complexity of the business model approach creates uncertainty as schools examine methods and philosophies, which will result in increased standardized test scores. Traditional attempts toward increased test scores include personnel development, changes in scheduling, curriculum restructuring, and homogeneous grouping (Boyles; Senge et al.). These attempts, reflecting a business

1

approach toward change, culminate with varied results and may not produce the long-term successes for which school leaders strive.

Existing empirical evidence suggests a focus on organizational culture to increase business outcomes (Collins, 2004; Peters & Waterman, 1982). Researchers concluded that organizations making a shift from traditional management approaches to a focus on culture have improved various aspects of the organization including profits, employee morale, and shared knowledge (Bagraim, 2001; Denison & Mishra, 1989; Detert, 2000; Heskett & Kotter, 1992). Given the importance for increased achievement in schools, knowledge of school culture may allow school leaders to understand the influence of culture on measurable outcomes (Deal & Peterson, 1999a).

Problem Statement

Standardized test scores provide an approach to measuring school success similar to accounting practices used in business demonstrating a corporate mentality and production-line oriented process (Boyles, 2000). Although empirical evidence suggests that organizational culture influences measurable business outcomes, research on the concept of school culture and culture's influence on measurable school outcomes is limited (Collins, 2004; Collins & Porras, 1997; Deal & Kennedy, 1982; Detert, 2000; Hall & Hord, 2001; Heskett & Kotter, 1992; Schein, 1992).

The existing situation is that school leaders measure success as student achievement through performance on standardized tests and expect quantifiable outcomes, much like business leaders use quantitative data to measure business success (Boyles, 2000). Although it is the current paradigm of achievement, standardized testing is essentially a snapshot of student ability, which may fail to recognize adequately the essence of student potential, growth, or achievement in all academic subjects (Boyles, 2000; Olson, 2005; Wilson, 2005). Although standardized test scores measure student achievement, student achievement is influenced by school culture (Stolp & Smith, 1995). While business success is often quantifiable by dollar returns on products, and can be quantified without factoring in the business culture, the product of schools is the achievement of its human capital, students (Boyles, 2000). Failure to study school culture as influential to student outcomes may limit academic growth and may have serious consequences to overall school success as measured by testing. According to current research, cultural aspects of the school community should be considered in curriculum development, social initiatives, long-term academic planning, and student enrollment and screening procedures (Peterson, 2002). Lack of acknowledgement in these specific areas may allow culture to emerge without control; hence the school leadership and administration may be helpless to observe culture rather than direct culture. Without directing culture, administrators may be unable to guide the academic practices of the school thus influencing student achievement and success at every school level. School administrators in several schools, along with other researchers (Craig et al., 2005; Reavis, Vinson, & Fox, 1999) have reported that a focus on culture has increased student outcomes greatly and that culture is a common characteristic of high-performing schools. This study was designed to be similar to studies by Heskett and Kotter (1992); Collins and Porras (1997); and Kotter, Sasser, and Schlesinger (1997) measuring organizational culture to outcomes (Rollins & Roberts, 1998). This quantitative correlation study was designed to determine whether perceived school culture related to student achievement as

3

measured by standardized test scores in a population of 17 elementary and secondary schools located in southwestern Arizona.

Background

Much debate exists over the use of standardized tests as the measure of school success (Boyles, 2000). Proponents point to research studies that indicate that state accountability systems with standardized tests attached have resulted in improved results on standardized tests and general school achievement measures (Protheroe & Perkins-Gough, 2001). Critics claim that limiting the scope of achievement or improvement to performance on standardized testing does not clearly indicate educational improvement and narrows the focus of a rich, fulfilling education experience to basic skill competency (McNeil, 2000b).

Legislation, including the No Child Left Behind Act of 2001, has created a scenario of accountability, or the measure of school success, for school districts based upon standardized test scores. Scores are obtained via delivery and completion of a state-mandated exam (Boyles, 2000; Fritzberg, 2004; Kucerik, 2002). These exams are norm referenced or criterion-referenced. Norm referenced exams are based upon the mean score for previous attempts at the test (Harcourt Assessment, Inc., 2004). The means of the previous year form the expected mean for the following year. Criterion-referenced exams examine specific material or skills attained by the learner. Criterion-referenced tests measure absolute or specific levels of achievement and are not dependent upon the scores of previous test takers, which is the basis of norm-referenced testing (Vogt, 1999).

State educational regulators evaluate schools for sanctions, so it would be useful for school officials to boost the average test score for each individual school and school

4

district, as their personal careers and the future of the school are dependent upon those

actions (Sacks, 1999). Standardized testing programs measure the progress and

shortcomings of education, or at least in theory, and the ensuing reports form the opinions

of parents and public officials (Nelson, Carlson, & Palonsky, 1996; Queen, 1999). Many

factors contribute to test score results, including poverty, leadership, communication,

educational disadvantage and opportunity, and school culture (Senge et al., 2000).

Determining, diagnosing, and analyzing school culture may allow school leaders to direct

and plan staff development and training around school culture issues. Improving school

culture may have an influential relationship on standardized test scores as the measure of

school success (Deal & Peterson, 1999b).

Measuring school success based upon the scores of standardized testing creates a

mechanistic approach similar to that in business (Boyles, 2000). Although the school

community appears content with current practice, the accountability to government

agencies looms overhead because of concerns regarding taxpayer money, school quality,

student employability, and the ability to perform basic skills outside the school setting

(McNeil, 2000a).

Regardless of current school practice, schools must meet the standards set forth

by legislation such as the No Child Left Behind Act of 2001 (U.S. Department of

Education, 2002). Many schools are attaining high levels, or performing well, on

standardized tests; however, those schools that are not may desire to consider an

approach to change, or a diagnosis of current performance. Deal and Peterson (1999a,

1999b) explained that school cultures that value collegiality, professionalism, and shared

learning create a positive scenario where information is exchanged freely. Many businesses have analyzed organizational culture to determine approaches toward change and to increase organizational performance, and schools may benefit from a similar approach (Collins & Porras, 1997; Denison & Mishra, 1989; Detert, 2000; Morgan, 1998; Trice & Beyer, 1993).

Purpose of the Study

The purpose of this quantitative study was to discover the perceptions of school culture and correlate those perceptions with standardized test scores in elementary and secondary schools in southwestern Arizona. To examine this relationship, participating school districts and individual schools in southwestern Arizona were surveyed using the School Culture Survey (Leithwood, Aitken, & Jantzi, 2001). This survey examined aspects of school culture, including the strength of relationships, forms of professional collaboration, climate of the physical environment, student-centered learning, and the professional work environment. The quantitative survey research method selected was appropriate to this study because the study quantified school organizational culture and student achievement test data. Once quantified, the results were correlated to discover if a relationship existed.

The independent variable in this study was school organizational culture, which was determined by the use of the School Culture Survey by Leithwood et al. (2001). Survey results were analyzed using descriptive statistics to determine a mean. The dependent variable was standardized test scores measured by the Stanford Achievement Test: Ninth Edition (SAT-9) published by Harcourt Assessment, Inc., and distributed by the Arizona Department of Education (2004). Scores from the 2003–2004 school year were the only scores considered. The SAT-9 scores for the study comprised Grades 2–12, depending on particular grades in each school, as some schools were elementary and others secondary. Grade participation per school was not described because that information would allow the reader to distinguish SAT-9 scores and school culture scores of participating schools and could compromise the anonymity of participants. The scores were compiled to reach a mean score.

The population of the study was comprised of teachers and principals in 17 elementary and secondary schools in southwestern Arizona. The geographic location of the study was limited to southwestern Arizona. The existing elementary and secondary schools in Yuma County and two elementary schools bordering Yuma County were solicited to participate in the study. Seventeen of 35 possible schools, 5 years or older, agreed to participate in the study. Teachers, resident speech therapists, school psychologists and other related personnel, principals, and assistant principals were invited to participate in the study.

Significance of the Study

The significance of this study rests in the knowledge that research on school culture and measurable outcomes is limited. A focus on school culture can increase student outcomes; positive school culture is a common characteristic of high-performing schools (Craig et al., 2005; Reavis Vinson, & Fox, 1999). Given that educational accountability focuses upon the scores of standardized testing as the measure of school success, this study was developed to establish the relationship between school culture and standardized test scores (Carnegie Council on Adolescent Development, 1989; Murphy & Louis, 1999). Deal and Peterson (1999a, 1999b) explained that research on the concept of culture and the influence of culture on measurable outcomes is significant in business

organizations but is relatively new as a philosophy in public schools.

Similar research regarding student achievement has included (a) poverty, (b)

financial resources or per pupil expenditures, (c) teacher quality, and (d) language issues

or second language learners. The idea of culture as a significant influence on student

achievement only recently has been examined (Deal & Peterson, 1999a). Empirical

evidence suggests the culture of a business organization can influence productivity;

hence, there is reason to believe similar cultural dimensions accounting for increased

business performance may account for increased achievement in schools (Deal &

Peterson, 1999a).

Significance to Leadership

This study contributes to the field of organizational leadership by increasing the

awareness of school administrators to view organizational culture as a significant

contributor to organizational success (student achievement as measured by standardized

tests). Schein (1992) explained, "Leadership is intertwined with cultural formation" (p.

316).

This study also contributed to the body of leadership knowledge by discovering

the perceptions of school culture and the relationship between culture and measurable

student outcomes. This model of accountability resembles the business model of

measurable results. According to federal and state legislative bodies, the highest levels of

excellence in student achievement and teachers' instruction appeal to common sense in

that they posit that the matter of quality education is an easy thing to measure and that

results will be readily achievable through testing, testing, and more testing, complemented by a system of sanctions and rewards. In this system, there will be no room for inadequacy for students, teachers, and principals, as the measurements for learning are similar to measurement in business (Boyles, 2000).

Nature of the Study

A correlation study examined the relationship between school organizational culture and the scores on standardized tests as the measure of school success in elementary and secondary schools in southwestern Arizona. A survey was determined the best measure of culture, because the survey to be used (a) quantified school organizational culture and (b) did not require a venue where the researcher and participant would work simultaneously to complete the questionnaire, which would allow the researcher to survey participants without supervision.

Quantitative methods, specifically the use of surveys, are occasionally employed in education research (Smith & Glass, 1987). The quantitative approach uses strategies of inquiry, such as experiments and surveys, and collects data on predetermined instruments, which yield statistical data (Creswell, 2003). As a method, the survey is a research tool in which a sample of subjects is drawn from a population and studied (often interviewed) in order to make inferences about the population. This design contrasts with the true experiment, in which subjects are assigned randomly to conditions or treatments. Surveys in education may measure school culture, school leadership, student motivation, teacher quality, or any other number of education-related ideas (Vogt, 1999).

The School Culture Survey (Leithwood et al., 2001) measures school culture and allows the results to be quantified to a mean score. The SAT-9 (Harcourt Assessment, Inc., 2004) was determined to be the best student achievement test because (a) the SAT is

9

used by all schools in the studies geographical area; (b) the test is normed; and (b) compared to other tests used within the state, the SAT-9 is more reliable regarding the consistency of results and information available to school districts and the public at large (Melendez & Konig, 2004). This design allows the reader to view the perceptions of school culture and compare those perceptions to current standardized test scores.

Research Questions

To complete this research study, a quantitative research method was employed to answer the following questions:

1. What are the mean culture scores measured by the School Culture Survey for participating schools?

2. What are the mean standardized test scores in language arts, reading, and mathematics as measured by the Stanford Achievement Test, Ninth Edition, (SAT-9) for participating schools?

3. Is there a relationship between school organizational culture as measured by the School Culture Survey and the results of standardized test scores in language arts, reading, and mathematics as measured by the Stanford Achievement Test, Ninth Edition (SAT-9)?

Hypothesis

Based on the research questions, a hypothesis was developed for this study. The hypothesis predicted there would be a significant relationship between a school's organizational culture and the results of standardized test scores in language arts, reading, and mathematics as measured by the SAT-9.

Theoretical Framework

The theoretical framework for this dissertation was based on the concept of culture in organizations and that culture's relation to increased, measurable success. Culture is described in this study and viewed from a historical perspective through definitions and descriptions from common terminology, within schools, through diagnosis and analysis and through the concept of cultural capital (Barrett, 2003). Culture theory holds roots in anthropology and social psychology (Schein, 1992). According to Trice and Beyer (1993), the first study of culture within organizations occurred in the 1930s. This occurred during the last phase of the Hawthorne studies at the Western Electric Company in Chicago. Experiments in this study focused upon the relationship between productivity and the physical work environment. Mayo (1927) was the researcher for this study, but employed an anthropologist named W. Lloyd Warner. Mayo argued that Warner could adapt the anthropological methods employed to uncover the social structures and belief systems in tribal societies to the work community at Western Electric. The study described three kinds of relationships: (a) technical, (b) social, and (c) ideological. Technical relationships concerned the flow of materials. Social relationships regarded the hierarchy of work distribution known as formal, and the friendships and cliques created in an informal manner. Ideological relationships concerned culture, which was constructed of shared beliefs and understandings within the work setting (Trice & Beyer).

The study of organizational culture became more important with the increase of global competition in business (Rollins & Roberts, 1998). American business practice differed from business practice in other countries significantly with respect to culture.

Awareness of culture and the increased concern to understand the function of how organizations worked rather than the structure of the organization amplified the acknowledgement of culture as a significant factor in organizations (Collins & Porras, 1997; Heskett & Kotter, 1992; Pondy & Mitroff, 1979; Rollins & Roberts).

Schein (1992) defined culture as the following:

A pattern of shared basic assumptions that the group learned as it solved its problems of external adaptation and internal integration, which has worked well enough to be considered valid and, therefore, to be taught to new members as the correct way to perceive, think, and feel in relation to those problems. (p. 12)

Considering the historical background discussed by Trice and Beyer (1993) and the definition of culture provided by Schein (1992), school culture was defined by Stolp and Smith (1995) as historically transmitted patterns of meaning that included the norms, values, beliefs, traditions, and myths understood, maybe in varying degrees, by members of the school community. Deal and Peterson (1999a) discussed schools as complex webs of traditions created by students, parents, community, and school staff through working together, solving problems, and sharing accomplishments. Deal and Peterson (1999a) and Stolp and Smith discussed current approaches to organizational culture in schools, and recognized that historically the term *climate* was used to describe the cultural setting in schools. *Culture*, however, describes the concept with more accuracy, entailing aspects of the setting including traditions, values, norms, beliefs, celebrations, language, and the social relationships regarding friendship and work (Hall & Hord, 2001).

Definitions

Research regarding school organizational culture and standardized test scores as the measure of school success requires the study of commonly identified terms of organizational culture and student performance assessment. A clear understanding of these terms will increase the effectiveness of this study.

Adequately Yearly Progress (AYP): The Arizona Department of Education (2004) defined *AYP* as the level of proficiency students must achieve in mathematics, reading, and writing.

Culture: According to Schein (1992), culture is a pattern of shared basic assumptions that the group or organization learned as it solved its problems of external adaptation and internal integration, that has worked well enough to be considered valid and, therefore, to be taught to new members as the correct way to perceive, think, and feel in relation to those problems.

Measure of Academic Progress (MAP): The Arizona Department of Education (2004) defined *measure of academic progress* as goals derived from the use of SAT-9 stanines and used to measure individual student growth.

No Child Left Behind Act of 2001: The No Child Left Behind Act is federal legislation designed to strengthen accountability for results, expand local control, expand options for parents, and emphasize teaching methods proven to work. This federal legislation requires that states develop performance-based standards in reading and mathematics. Then, each state educational agency must implement a system of annual testing, which will determine if standards are being achieved. Data from these tests must be made available as public record and published in school report cards and local newspapers (Kucerik, 2002; U.S. Department of Education, 2002).

One Year's Growth (OYG): The Arizona Department of Education (2004) defined *OYG* as attaining the same stanine score or a higher stanine score on the SAT-9 than the previous year.

Percentile rank: Percentile ranks reflect a percentage compared to other schools, classes or students taking the test. If a school score is 39, it means that the average student at this school scored better than 39% of the students in the norming group. This study used school-wide scores for correlation with school culture means (Arizona Department of Education, 2004).

Stanford Achievement Test: Ninth Edition (SAT-9): The SAT-9 is a norm-referenced test developed by Harcourt Brace Publishing (Harcourt Assessment, Inc., 2004) and taken by students throughout the state of Arizona. The test examines language, reading, and mathematics and makes comparisons to other schools on a national level.

Stanine: Stanines are standard scores that range from a low of 1 to a high of 9, with 5 being designated average performance. National stanines, like national percentile ranks, indicate a student's relative standing in the national norm group (Arizona Department of Education, 2004).

Assumptions

An assumption of this study regarded the honest response of subjects to the questions of the survey regarding school culture. Honest information from the survey would ensure adequate culture designations for participating schools and provide a clear picture of the school culture mean for correlation to standardized testing data. The availability of standardized testing data corresponded with the collection of survey information, and the data were assumed to be correct and aligned to the performance of participating schools. The data from standardized testing were available as information in the public domain from the Arizona Department of Education (n.d.) Web site.

Scope, Limitations, and Delimitations

The scope of this study was public school principals and teachers in 17 elementary and secondary schools and school districts in southwestern Arizona. Geographically, this study was limited to schools and school districts within southwestern Arizona. The results can be generalized to other populations, if similar circumstances are evident including ethnicity, economics, school size, and performance on standardized tests. The items used in the survey were the only indicators of culture, and the survey was administered to teachers and administrators. Other cultural factors, including parent and student perceptions, outside school activities, and extracurricular activities, were not considered. The research was limited to the test score results determined by the SAT-9 (Harcourt Assessment, Inc., 2004) for the 2003–2004 school year.

This study was restricted to the responses of teachers and administrators employed in participating schools during the 2003–2004 school year. Teacher and principal perceptions of culture are sufficient for this study, rather than student or parent perceptions, for example, because most of the schools are 4-year schools, and a goal of the study was to discover perceptions of culture of individuals who had been in the school setting for at least 5 years. This study discovered perceptions of school culture and the relationship between those perceptions and standardized test scores.

Summary

Chapter 1 provided a statement of the problem and an explanation of the purpose and significance of the study, including an overview of school culture, organizational culture, and the significance of school success, as measured by standardized testing. School organizational culture influences every part of the educational setting and creates an environment for the exchange of social and professional ideas (Deal & Peterson, 1999a). Sergiovanni (2000) expressed similar thoughts for schools as communities of individuals building culture through trust and shared values. Empirical evidence suggests the culture of a business organization can influence productivity; hence, there is reason to believe similar cultural dimensions accounting for increased business performance may account for increased achievement in schools (Deal & Peterson, 1999a). Chapter 2 will provide relevant literature regarding the problem of this study with respect to corporate culture and measurable success, school organizational culture, and the influence of culture on leadership. Chapter 3 will describe the design and the methods of gathering data for this study. Chapter 4 will discuss the findings of the research, summarize, and analyze the information acquired. Chapter 5 finalizes the research with the author's conclusions and recommendations.

CHAPTER 2: LITERATURE REVIEW

The purpose of this quantitative study was to discover the perceptions of school organizational culture and correlate those perceptions with standardized test scores in elementary and secondary schools in southwestern Arizona. Standardized test score results provide a mechanistic approach to measuring the service and delivery of instruction in schools, which is an approach resembling a corporate or business model (Boyles, 2000). Empirical evidence suggests that a focus on culture has allowed business leaders to increase measures of business success including profits, stock value, human capital, job satisfaction and commitment and other business related matters (Chen, 2004; Collins, 2004; Collins & Porras, 1997; Denison & Mishra, 1989; Heskett & Kotter, 1992; Rollins & Roberts, 1998).

Title Searches, Research Documents, Journals, and Articles

This literature review, presented in five sections, discusses pertinent authors and case studies related to this dissertation. The first section focuses on definitions, descriptions, characteristics and examples of organizational culture and culture theory from select authors, and case studies that label, define, and recognize culture in researched organizations. The second section focuses on the elements of organizational culture and change in business practice. This section includes pertinent literature and case studies explaining how a focus on organizational culture can lead to measurable business improvement and success. The third section defines and explains the elements of organizational culture in the school setting. The fourth section discusses standardized testing and its importance in current school operation as the measure of school success.

The fifth and final section explores school leadership and its position regarding standardized testing and organizational culture and change.

A slight literature gap exists, as there is a great amount of literature on organizational culture and measurable outcomes, compared to a limited amount of literature on organizational culture in schools correlated to measurable outcomes. The significant literature in this field of research dates back to the 1980s and 1990s. Appendix A reveals the results of the title searches.

Organizational Culture

This portion of the literature review discusses definitions of organizational culture and case studies regarding the various terms and descriptors of organizational culture. These terms and definitions are similar to the terms and definitions of school culture.

Schein's (1985) conceptual model of organizational culture offered insight into the deeper understanding of culture. His work was representative of a variety of studies that described culture as a system of relationships and shared meanings. Schein defined culture as follows:

> Culture is a pattern of shared basic assumptions that the group learned as it solved its problems of external adaptation and internal integration that has worked well enough to be considered valid and, therefore, to be taught to new members as the correct way to perceive, think, and feel in relation to those problems. (p. 12)

Three significant, basic levels of culture are (a) artifacts, (b) espoused values, and (c) basic assumptions. The first, artifacts, are the visible and physical products and behaviors of an organization. Artifacts include all that one can see, hear, and feel in a new culture (Schein, 1992).

The second aspect is espoused values. Schein (1992) explained that espoused values are formed throughout the organization's lifetime. Original values, however, stem from an individual's original values for the organization. The individual may be the creator, leader, or organizer of the entity. The owner of a fast food restaurant may value speedy service and build all corporate ideas around that value. In contrast, a competitor may value delicious food and build the organization around that value. Values may outlast revolving leadership and frequent turmoil within the organization. Values that become embodied in an ideology or organizational philosophy may act as a guide when dealing with uncertainty and poor leadership, thus making values so important to the organization (Schein).

The third indicator of culture is basic underlying assumptions (Schein, 1992). Basic assumptions are the aspects of the organization that are taken for granted because they work without effort. An example is a school, which is designed to provide a service and not to turn a profit. The service is to educate; therefore, a basic assumption is that the service provided will teach all children attending the school to read. It is assumed that any business is in business to make money. Sports teams do not spend millions of dollars on players and marketing to lose every game. It is assumed the acquisition of players and the marketing of the game will draw fans to see a winning organization. Assumptions also build culture, because assumptions give the organization something personal, similar to an inside joke.

Artifacts, assumptions, and values are three very distinct aspects of culture. Internal relationships are also of great importance if an organization is to survive the external environment (Schein, 1992). To survive, a group must create a common

19

language that does not inhibit communication. The common language can be referred to as *jargon* (Schein). The organization must define membership. This includes how one joins and departs the organization. The rank and status of members must be decided and peer relationship guidelines established. Being a leader and how one becomes a leader are clear and well defined. Peer relations include romantic interests, outside contact, and general rules of engagement. The group defines rewards and punishment. The membership understands what will be rewarded and what will not be tolerated in the way of work. Finally, the unexplainable must be explained, because organizations usually like to control the influence of assumptions.

Six major characteristics of culture include (a) collective, (b) emotionally charged, (c) historically based, (d) dynamic, (e) inherently fuzzy, and (g) inherently symbolic (Trice & Beyer, 1993). Trice and Beyer described these six characteristics accordingly:

1. Collective culture refers to the production of culture among members of an organization and the adherence to the beliefs, values, and norms of that culture.

2. Cultures are emotionally charged because cultures manage, channel, and control emotions. The sharing of information, rites, and rituals within a culture contributes to emotional well-being or instability.

3. Cultures develop historically within organizations. Through shared experiences, decision making, and coping with political, economic, and social situations, cultures develop and create a foundation of decision-making.

4. Cultures continually change, creating a dynamic environment expressed through communication, change of membership, and the impact of external and internal forces.

5. Cultures are inherently fuzzy due to the complex and fragmented experiences of the organization's members.

6. Finally, cultures are symbolic, and symbolism has a role in communication and expression (Trice & Beyer, 1993)

Hatch (1997) explained that organizational culture is difficult to define. Historically, culture referred to the tending of crops and animals. Metaphorically, humans are tended to via the family unit, the community, educational institutions, and religious institutions. The association of culture with social progress, civilization, and aesthetic achievement including arts, sciences, and architecture added a sense of elitism to the definition. The addition of elitism to the definition of culture has created thought pertaining to high and low culture, or primitive and advanced culture. This thought leads to the idea of a successful culture or a failing culture, or the recognition of culture as the reason for success or failure in organizations.

Morgan (1998) expressed a similar view. The word *culture* is derived metaphorically from the term *cultivation*. Cultivation refers to the development and tending of land, thus culture refers to the tending of society. Organizational culture usually refers to the pattern of development reflected socially in knowledge, ideology, values, laws, and daily rituals. Through the cultural structure of the organization as a social reality, organizations become mini-societies creating culture through daily practice and operation. Organizations form local cultures of their own that are of significance for their functioning (Alveeson, 1990). Organizations appear deeper than the mechanistic description of a formal structure, instrument, or machine.

Culture implies a sense of intimacy, thus making the organization feel small to each member (Duques & Gaske, 1997). Duques and Gaske identified four elements to remaining small in the perception of organization members including: (a) maintaining clear articulation of and strong adherence to organizational values; (b) remaining accountable for employee and client satisfaction; (c) associating low levels of fear with innovation; and (d) associating security with earning, rather than having it be an entitlement. Intimacy within an organization contributes to respect and fitting in (Hanson & Lackman, 2001). Culture is more than shared social values, but the sharing of expectations and fulfilling appropriate social roles. These roles contribute to steady or uniform behavior and act as a control, often more influential than punishment (Morgan, 1998).

Bolman and Deal (1997) discussed the ideas of frames, explaining, "Frames are, essentially, a lens through which to view aspects of an organization, and identify culture" (p. 37). The first frame is human resources. The human resources frame identifies the needs, skills, and the importance of a trusting and caring climate within the organization. The second frame is the structural frame. Structure describes the organizational hierarchy, goals, and results. The third frame is the political frame. The political frame discusses the political pull of resources, conflict, power, negotiations, and cliques. The fourth and final frame is the symbolic. Symbols refer to the visual and recognizable aspects of culture including rituals, ceremonies, stories, and logos.

A case study of two organizational cultures presented three active types of culture and one passive type of culture, originating in anthropology (Altman & Baruch, 1998). The three active cultures are (a) hierarchal, (b) sectarian, and (c) market. The research revealed a passive culture designated as fatalistic. Altman and Baruch described and examined the culture of the Israeli Defense Forces divided between army, navy, air force, and Apollo, which was a defense manufacturer. The research also discussed the dimensions of the labels of hierarchal, sectarian, market and passive according to the analysis of each organization. The researchers discovered that the culture of each organization revealed "old times" of operation and language, which shaped culture. Additional research revealed the high level of professionalism of pilots attributing to corporate culture aspects of competition in the air force. The culture of the army emphasized personal working abilities and the importance of individual skill over teamwork within armored tank corps. This idea contrasted with the team concepts emphasized in the infantry units. The culture of the navy emphasizes tight regulation and interpersonal reaction because of the closeness on vessels. Each entity—army, navy, air force, and Apollo—represented more than one possible facet of culture, thus making exact labeling difficult but recognizable among divisions within each organization. These similar aspects of culture occur in the school setting within the common divisions of subjects, athletics, arts, and administration. Subject areas are similar to the army as personal abilities attribute to classroom success. Athletics and arts compete for the best students and resources, thus contributing to a corporate culture. Administration, including office staff, works closely with and relies on interpersonal relationships and knowledge to complete tasks (Altman & Baruch).

A case study of one organization discussed how culture can be recognized in the practice of an organization (C. Smith, 2000). The case study discussed the recognition of organizational culture as culture is embodied in the structures, mechanisms, and practices of an organization. C. Smith stated that cultures run deep within an organization and change constitutes a disruption in practice, but does not always change the true practices of the organization. Organizations are defined socially, characterized by constructed objects, the nature, and control of those objects, and the operational mechanisms, which manage those objects. Change, by management for example, constitutes new ideas or techniques toward operation, but does not clearly remove the historically aligned practices.

Organizational culture often reflects the values and vision of the organization's founder (Ogbonna, 2001). Ogbonna incorporated two case studies reviewing the strategic visions, objectives, and decisions of the founder and its influence on present-day organizational strategies. The organizations of the study were considerably small and family owned. Both organizations reflected practices based upon the strategies of the founder; however, at times the initial strategies were positive or negative toward current organizational practice. The initial strategies of the founder formulated and maintained a sense of culture in the organization despite the opportunity to move away from historical practice and negative consequences.

Organizational culture has been identified and analyzed by a number of authors (Alveeson, 1990; Deal & Kennedy, 1982; Geertz, 1973; Hatch, 1997; Morgan, 1998; Schein, 1992; Trice & Beyer, 1993). Authors and researchers concluded that *shared beliefs, decision making, values, experiences, rites,* and *rituals* are terms associated with the definition of organizational culture. Beyond the analysis and definition of the practices within an organization, empirical evidence suggests that culture can have a significant impact on organizational outcomes.

Organizational Culture and Measurable Outcomes

Significant literature regarding organizational culture was written throughout the 1980s and early 1990s. The literature described and analyzed organizational culture but made no significant correlation between culture and organizational outcomes. The validity of organizational culture described as good or excellent was questioned as ambiguous and not holding validity. Research followed examining the influence of culture in high-performing organizations and explored the relationships through scientific methods.

Denison and Mishra (1989) presented empirical evidence examining the relationship between organizational culture and organizational effectiveness from a sample of 969 organizations. First, the authors discussed four hypotheses regarding and defining culture including (a) involvement, (b) consistency, (c) adaptability, and (d) mission. The involvement hypothesis suggested that culture is created from a sense of ownership and responsibility. As organization members increase participation, organization performance increases. The consistency hypothesis emphasized that strong cultural aspects—including shared values, beliefs, and symbols—affect the organization's ability to reach consensus and coordinate activities. The hypothesis suggested that the cultural practice influences the organization over explicit rules and regulations. The adaptability hypothesis explained that organizations hold a system of norms and values, which supports the ability to learn as an organization and thus

25

increases survival, growth, and development. The final hypothesis, mission, provided meaning and purpose through the definition of a social role, concluding that culture is formed via the organization's function in society.

Denison and Mishra (1989) described effectiveness as the organization's ability to develop new products, grow sales, increase market share, increase cash flow, and increase return on assets. These terms are measured and quantified into a number representing overall performance. The authors analyzed the culture of each organization according to the four descriptors and correlated the quantified cultural finding with organizational outcomes. The study demonstrated that a culture representative of the mission hypothesis displayed the best overall performance. The study suggested that culture influenced organizational outcomes and that organizations may be defined by the four hypothesis described by the author. Denison and Mishra suggested that organizational leaders may consider the perceptions within the organization and redirect the organization away from current practice.

Heskett and Kotter (1992) summarized a wide range of quantitative research discussing the link between culture and performance. Studies were conducted between August 1987 and January 1991 to determine whether a relationship exists between corporate culture (organizational culture) and economic performance. Adaptive cultures, which contributed to continuous performance, focused on customers, employees, stockholders, and general organizational constituency. The studies incorporated organizations including Wal-Mart, Hewlett Packard, and PepsiCo. These organizations employed managers described as caring deeply about customers, employees, and stockholders and based decisions on the interests of these three groups. In contrast, organizations considered having low-performance cultures included three main

characteristics: (a) Managers showed by action that care was not given to customers,

employees, and stockholders; (b) managers appeared arrogant and unwilling to receive

input; and (c) the relationship between managers and leadership was hostile with regard

to change (Heskett & Kotter).

Research within the chosen corporations demonstrated that culture may not

always help corporations, but evidence from employees suggested that culture can hurt

organizations. Heskett and Kotter (1992) described as high performing those that

increased revenues, expanded the workforce, grew stock prices, and improved net

incomes. Firms considered higher performing scored higher on a culture index than those

considered low performing. Higher performing firms averaged a 6.1, with a 7 being the

highest, compared to low-performing firms, which averaged a 3.7 (Heskett & Kotter).

Collins and Porras (1997) studied 18 visionary companies over each company's

history and compared organizational culture to organizational outcomes regarding

performance related to revenue, employment, stock prices, and net income. The historical

significance of the study concluded that visionary companies tended to have cult-like

cultures. Descriptions of the companies included a strong ideology, solid indoctrination

of employees into core ideology, employees fitting into the organization, and a sense of

elitism. Collins and Porras identified five elements that created a core ideology and

stimulated progress: (a) culture, (b) audacious goals, (c) experimentation and

examination, (d) home-grown management, and (e) results not good enough.

Collins and Porras (1997) concluded that culture influences organizational

performance. Firms with high-performing cultures demonstrated growth in revenue, employment, stock prices, and net income significantly greater than those with low-performing cultures. The research concluded that companies with low-performing cultures still performed. The contrast lies with the measure of the performance being significantly greater in high-performing cultures compared to low-performing cultures.

Collins (2004) researched the idea of companies moving from "good to great." The research reviewed companies taking the leap to become the dominant force in a particular industry. Industries included electronics, automobiles, investing, and banking. Collins described the force of leadership and its strong impact on market performance. Businesses with overly strong leaders created a strong performing organization, and this strong performance was derived from stock performance, layoffs, market share, and corporate change.

Collins (2004) divided the researched companies into four sections. Each initial company appeared on the 1965, 1975, 1985, and 1995 *Fortune* magazine rankings, or "Fortune 500." The number for initial categorization of companies was 1,435 firms. These companies were further reduced to 126 firms based on research at the University of Chicago. The second cut was based upon rates of return and especially above average returns to investors over 10- to 15-year periods. The study further reduced 126 companies to 19 companies in the third cut. Companies were narrowed to 19 based on criteria including performance and consistency of performance over a period of time. Companies were eliminated if change occurred too fast or if the companies lacked breakthrough, changed from great to good, had incurred mergers, or had periods of good and bad returns.

Collins (2004) explained that culture contributed to organizational success, and that this success was significant with regard to leadership. Strong leadership guiding every facet of the company created success but not long-lasting success, thus creating a culture of dependence. Strong cultures survive change in the position of leadership, and culture influences the actions of the organization toward success compared to leadership steering. Collins explained that "good-to-great companies had Level 5 leaders who built an enduring culture of discipline, the unsustained comparisons had Level 4 leaders who personally disciplined the organization through sheer force" (p. 130).

According to Barret (2003), companies that actively seek to align the values of the organization with the values of employees (and vice versa) are more successful because they are focused on the needs of the employees and customers. Organizations that do not have this alignment tend to be more inward looking, bureaucratic, and stressful toward organization members. Although these organizations may be financially successful, finding and retaining talented people proves difficult.

The first step in creating values alignment is to carry out an assessment of current culture. Based on this information, organizations are able to choose core values, which are meaningful to all employees. In addition to the values alignment, it is possible to use this method to measure cultural entropy within the organization. Cultural entropy is the amount of energy consumed by the people in an organization that is not available for useful, productive work. Cultural entropy increases when there is bureaucracy, internal competition, information hoarding, and blame (Barret, 2003).

The degree of cultural entropy in a corporate culture is measured by looking at the proportion of votes for potentially limiting values (Barret, 2003). Barret found that low-entropy organizations strongly correlate with high values alignment, and organizations displaying both these characteristics—low entropy and a high number of matching values—were the healthiest, most resilient, and the most profitable among researched organizations.

Research conducted on more than 600 value assessments concluded that a company with a high degree of values alignment never displayed high entropy, and a company with a high degree of values alignment was always financially successful (Barret, 2003). The best of the best, from a performance perspective, always have a high degree of values alignment, positive values at every level of organizational consciousness, and low levels of entropy (Barret).

A case study of European firms explained that the cultural influence created by the founders of the organization can have long-lasting influence on organizational outcomes (Miller, 2004). Globally, CEOs have rediscovered business principles, including focusing on what a company does best, eschewing fads, and creating an ethical corporate culture with the power to guide inspire. Thomson Financial created a unique index for both family and nonfamily firms in European countries. These companies were tracked for over 10 years through December 2003. Thomson Financial also produced a list of the top 10 fastest growing family company stocks in Europe. In Germany, the family index soared 206%, led by BMW, while the nonfamily stocks climbed just 47%. In France, the family index surged an equally breathtaking 203%, led by the likes of Sanofi-Synthelab, L'Oreal, and L. V. M. H. Indeed, this analysis runs counter to recent headline-grabbing scandals, which portray family businesses as a confederacy of scoundrels. Thompson Financial concluded that it is no coincidence that family companies are particularly strong in France, which is described as the epicenter of the mass-luxury trend (Miller).

Culture can have a significant influence on internal factors within organizations, thus reinforcing the importance of culture in organizations. Research exists suggesting culture has influential outcomes on organizational concerns, including human resources, innovation, productivity, and organizational change.

Culture influences measurable data within organizations, including job satisfaction and commitment. Chen (2004) studied the effect of organizational culture on organizational commitment, job satisfaction, and job performance. This quantitative study surveyed 84 small and mid-sized firms in Taiwan. Chen concluded that organizational culture positively correlated with job satisfaction, and commitment but not significantly with job performance. The study suggests that culture influences commitment and satisfaction but has no influence on the performance of that job.

The preceding studies of corporate, organizational culture described issues similar to those studied in this research. The influence of culture may have a significant influence on organizational outcomes, innovation, and measurable success. The organizations studied displayed strong cultures, described by aligned values, shared vision, and common goals. These strong cultures influence and are correlated with measurable organizational success. Schools and businesses hold significant differences but are measured in nearly the same manner (Boyles, 2000). Standardized test score outcomes are the current measure of school success, and these scores can be quantified and compared. The following section describes and defines school organizational culture and discusses case studies correlating school culture and school outcomes.

School Culture

The concept of schools having distinctive cultures dates back to the 1930s. Waller discussed the idea of school organizational culture in 1932 as follows:

Schools have a culture that is definitely their own. There are, in the school, complex rituals of personal relationships, a set of folkways, mores, and irrational sanctions, a moral code based upon them. There are games, which are sublimated wars, teams, and an elaborate set of ceremonies concerning them. There are traditions, and traditionalists waging their world-old battle against innovators. (p. 96)

Of the many different conceptions of culture, none is universally accepted as the one best definition. One scholar defined culture as the web of significance in which we all are suspended (Geertz, 1973). Another suggested simply that culture is "the way we do things around here" or the shared beliefs and values that closely knit a community together. Deal and Peterson (1999b) described culture as follows:

This invisible, taken-for-granted flow of beliefs and assumptions gives meaning to what people say and do. It shapes how they interpret hundreds of daily transactions. This deeper structure of life in organizations is reflected and transmitted through symbolic language and expressive action. Culture consists of the stable underlying social meanings that shape beliefs and behavior over time. (p. 3)

School culture affects and influences every part of the organization from what is discussed in the lunchroom, to the type of curriculum instruction that is valued, to the way students are envisioned and treated (Deal & Peterson, 1999b). According to Deal and Peterson (1999b), strong, positive, collaborative cultures have the following six

powerful effects on the school organization:

1. Culture fosters effectiveness and productivity.

2. Culture improves collegial and collaborative activities that foster better

communication and problem-solving practices.

3. Culture fosters successful change and improvement efforts.

4. Culture builds commitment and identification of staff, students, and

administrators.

5. Culture amplifies the energy, motivation, and vitality of a school staff,

students, and community.

6. Culture increases the focus of daily behavior and attention on what is

important and valued.

Similar to the ideas of Deal and Peterson, Stolp and Smith (1995) defined school

culture as historically transmitted patterns of meaning that include the norms, values,

beliefs, traditions, and myths understood, maybe in varying degrees, by members of the

school community. Educators speak of school culture as "the way we do things around

here," and the same assumptions continue to shape how people think about their work,

relate to their colleagues, define their mission, and derive their sense of identity.

Cultural theory is based on the axiom that what matters to most people is their

relationships with other people (Perkinson, 1995). According to cultural theory,

individuals follow and act in ways, which support a personal preferred way of life.

Education in the United States has reflected several cultural ideas including hierarchies,

Christian service, and egalitarian. Hierarchs believed that specialization and the division of labor allowed people to live together harmoniously. Educators believed Christian moral values would restore American culture and reduce social disorder. Egalitarians believed education would create an equal society where conditions were normed for all students and then all adults.

Marriot (2001) suggested that culture is evident in school pride, open communication, productivity, cooperation, widespread involvement, a sense of cohesiveness, and acts of caring and sharing. School organizational culture is also related to accomplished teaching and powerful learning, which are the hallmarks of effective schools.

The impact of school culture is not surprising, considering that school culture defines the social, emotional, cognitive, and physical context within which the school community functions (Marriot, 2001). Observers of current education practice may find it surprising that in this time of increased public and political scrutiny into issues of accountability, attention to school culture has been neglected. High academic standards, rigorous assessment of student achievement, and teacher preparation have been cast as the dominant components of current educational reform agendas. No educational reform will take root unless the reform is grounded in a positive and productive school organizational culture (Marriot).

Hall and Hord (2001) described culture as "the individually and socially constructed values, norms, and beliefs about an organization and how it should behave that can be measured only by observation of the setting using qualitative methods" (p. 66). Empirical evidence, however, regarding productive school district and individual school organizational cultures is limited to only a handful of studies. Schools in the

Sweetwater Union High School District in San Diego have changed the culture

throughout all schools district wide (Holmes, 2003). Students are making progress but not

in the name of a zero defect mentality to improve student achievement test results by

riding principals and school administrators at each grading quarter. In this school district,

Superintendent Edward Brand has led a cultural transformation. He has enlisted

principals, teachers, and even students in school leadership teams to carry the vision of

higher student achievement forward.

Similar to other California school districts, Sweetwater uses the state-mandated

SAT-9 to measure student academic progress. The test is one of 15 criteria used to judge

student performance and engage school staff in ongoing dialogue regarding student

achievement. This collaborative, team learning effort was designed to change and

transform the culture of the school district and ensure that as school district staff enter

and leave, district focus remains constant (Holmes, 2003).

Underneath the operating network of roles as teachers, classified staff, and

administrators lies a deep, less visible structure labeled *culture* (Goldring, 2002). Culture

is part of every group of people gathered together, whether work groups, neighborhoods,

schools, or large corporations. The power of culture lies in the ability to dictate

everything about a group, from what it discusses to the beliefs group members hold in

common and the values taught among group members. Culture is a visible and usable

tool in schools, because relationships tend to hold more power compared to official roles

and titles.

Results of a recent survey involving teachers and principals in a sample of

California schools agreed with the literature that culture is an effective tool, which is critical to the success of students (Goldring, 2002). A recent study of high schools in northern and central California involving students achieving beyond the level of similar schools concurred with earlier findings reported from educators about the strength of school culture. High schools selected for the study represented mid-size, urban, and large cities in five counties. The study surveyed teachers and principals of five comprehensive high schools selected from a population that matched the following criteria: (a) less than 50% of the student population was classified as White and non-Hispanic, (b) 40% or more of the students received free or reduced-price meals and/or CalWorks assistance, and (c) the school demonstrated 2 years of improved Academic Performance Index (API) scores by earning an API score of 600 or above in the year 2000 (Goldring).

In the study, teachers and principals were asked to prioritize which traits of culture most affected student achievement and to provide additional details about personal experience of each trait at school. Educators in the chosen schools experienced success evidenced by API scores surpassing 600, which is a remarkable difference from schools of similar populations. Principals were asked anonymously to assign teachers as proponents or opponents of change in a model originally used in corporations, and the priorities of these two groups were compared with those of principals (Goldring, 2002).

The results of the individual and combined studies offered some valuable information to site leaders (Goldring, 2002):

1. Teachers and principals across all school levels spoke with a single voice: The presence and use of a shared vision as a unifying factor uses the strength of school culture to affect student achievement.

2. Schools do not require 100% of their staff members to react positively toward change in order to continue working on reform issues.

3. The strengths and weaknesses within each trait area and the network of their connection at the school is a valuable source of information for site leaders.

4. The traits valued vary according to roles and, without discussion, may continue to misunderstanding.

Thus, Goldring's (2002) study stressed the importance of culture as the focus of leadership toward an understanding of student achievement. A case study by Shann (1999) attested to the importance of school culture for school effectiveness. Regarding cultures relationship to academic achievement, this study discussed prosocial and antisocial student behaviors as rated by 1,503 students and 92 teachers in four urban middle schools ranked in order by achievement. The highest achieving school combined an emphasis on academics with a culture of caring reflected in higher rates of prosocial behaviors. The second-ranked school of the study emulated a law-and-order type of environment, which did not contain the synergy of a caring community. The study concluded that creating a community of caring actually may be a necessary condition for maximal school achievement.

Teachers, traditionally, work independently without collaborating with their colleagues to improve student learning in a school wide environment. Changing this mindset to create a collaborative school culture is a challenge for the best principals but is possible with certain characteristics. Taylor (2002) discussed aspects of collaboration including trust, data-driven decision making, and celebrations. Trust was described as the most beneficial aspect of the teacher principal relationship. Teachers need to build trust with principals and with one another to collaborate on student learning in an authentic manner. Data-driven decision making is a concept based on recorded data, including student standardized achievement test scores. The data are analyzed to make decisions regarding staff, class sizes, and strategic planning. Celebrations are an important aspect of building culture. Celebrating success with sincerity is an important responsibility of school leadership.

As schools scramble to meet the stringent demands of high-stakes testing, researchers have attempted to identify the most important factors in creating collaborative, professional cultures for learning. A growing number of studies have provided rich descriptions of schools that support student achievement. A 3-year study by Strahan (2003) examined the dynamics of school culture in three elementary schools improving low-income and minority student achievement. From 1997 to 2002, student scores on state achievement tests rose from less than 50% proficient to more than 75% proficient. Research teams in the study constructed case studies by collecting demographic and achievement data, interviewing teachers and administrators, and observing lessons and meetings in each school. They reexamined data from three schools from an original case study to explore the professional culture of these particular schools due to 25% achievement test growth. Analysis of 51 original interviews and 28 new interviews indicated that personnel at these schools reported developing supportive cultures that enabled participants to coordinate efforts to improve instruction and strengthen professional learning communities (Strahan).

Many schools connect with the heart and soul of generations of students and continue to convey the promise of education for future generations (Glickman, 2003).

State and national education leaders were interviewed to discuss school cultures meeting

the following criteria: (a) a history of 10 to 30 years of sustained reform consistent with

the school's initial core values; (b) progressive education, characterized by participatory

learning, team structures, links between school community, performance-based

assessment, and inclusive, heterogeneous placement of students; (c) operation under the

governance of a school district, with the same funding and student enrollment as other

schools in the district; and (d) documented student results better than those of comparable

schools on a wide range of measures, including student test scores, student performances

and demonstrations, success in later life, lower dropout rates, and parent and student

satisfaction.

Glickman (2003) discovered 20 schools reflecting the ethnic, geographic, and

economic diversity of the United States. The schools chosen in the study contained an

intergenerational faculty and emulated an organization based on democratic ideals.

Rituals, activities, attitudes, purpose, and student achievement in each school reflected a

sense of sacredness for the community. The culture of each school was a historical

reflection, which led to students' experiencing a rich cultural atmosphere and heightened

academic experience.

According to Tobergte and Curtis (2002), school improvement, especially a focus

on academic achievement, begins with the transformation of school organizational

culture. School improvement begins with development of people and the school culture

to keep the organization vibrant and prepared to meet new needs and challenges. School

improvement involves recognizing the need for change, understanding the change, and

building support structures, which lead to comprehensive change and collective school improvement. Tobergte and Curtis described five behaviors leading to school improvement and the transformation of school culture: (a) building relationships within the culture that already exists, (b) recognizing the need for school improvement, (c) understanding the change process, (d) proactively developing the people and culture by creating a new focus, and (e) learning from past mistakes instead of dwelling on success.

Lucas, Quinn, Miles, Valentine, and Gawerecki (2002) described a collaborative culture and leadership transformation through six steps:

1. Developing vision is leadership identifying new opportunities and developing, articulating, and inspiring others with that vision.

2. Modeling behavior is setting an example for others to follow consistent with espoused leadership values.

3. Fostering commitment is leadership promoting cooperation in assisting members in working toward common goals.

4. Individualized support is leadership indicating respect for members and concern about personal feelings and needs.

5. Intellectual stimulation is leadership challenging members to reexamine their assumptions about their work and how it is done.

6. High expectation is described as leadership conveying an idea about excellence, quality, and high performance on the part of members.

Reavis et al. (1999) discussed cultural change in an underperforming school through motivation and example. Cottontown High School increased student passing rates on the state mandated exam from 38% to 87% for sophomores within a school year. This change occurred due to a focus on culture as the most influential factor in student motivation and achievement. The administrator created a system of rewards for all

employees, and students encompassing the established values of the school as an

organization.

Craig et al. (2005) explored high-performing schools throughout Tennessee. Their

study confirmed that one characteristic of high-performing schools is organizational

culture. The study used qualitative interview data from teachers and administrators in the

top 10% of schools throughout the state according to test scores. Craig et al.'s results

suggested that high expectations of quality, continuous professional development, and a

focus on community contributed to increased student achievement.

The case studies and literature selections reviewed school culture and the

influence of school culture on school outcomes. School culture reflects terms and

identifiers similar to culture in business and corporations. The following section reviews

the importance and influence of standardized test scores in current education practice.

Standardized Testing as the Measure of Success

This portion of the literature review discusses current aspects and writings

regarding standardized testing. Currently, standardized achievement tests are used to

measure school success. Schools are labeled according to test performance by federal and

state standards, and these labels are the foundation for school planning, hiring, and

instructional practice.

Currently in public education, standardized testing tends to drive the curriculum,

and teachers focus studies on these tests' subjects (Queen, 1999). No teacher desires for

students to perform poorly on standardized achievement tests, and no school

administrator wants his or her school to be ranked below others in the standard district

41

(Nelson et al., 1996). Teachers, administrators, parents, and local business leaders know that newspapers report the results of statewide testing, thus creating public perception regardless of alternate successes and failures. To avoid invidious comparisons, instruction is geared to the test. Ultimately, material not tested tends not to be taught, and this is especially true with courses in arts and sciences. Teachers and administrators fall victim to test makers' promises and the public's misplaced faith in testing (Sacks, 1999).

Nationwide testing has become a national obsession. In 1991, encouraged by Bill Clinton, then governor of Arkansas, and President George Bush, the education community began to develop standards into five core subjects (U.S. Department of Education, 2002). Test makers rushed tests to the market, and a national system of assessment was touted as a means to chart the progress of schools on the march to new higher standards. Recent articles in the *Yuma Sun* and the *Arizona Republic* newspapers stressed the importance of test scores as the measure of school success. The article in the *Yuma Sun* interviewed local principals on the reasons for performing low in each subject area on the test compared to other local schools. Principals of schools performing high, compared to other schools, were rarely interviewed. The article gave the name of each low-performing school and stressed the achievement test scores, regardless of other activities that might be considered successful at each school site (Leatherman, 2004). A similar article in the *Arizona Republic* stressed that scores in mathematics for Phoenix area schools were competitive or greater than the national average. Although the mathematics scores were considered impressive, low reading and language scores were noted for local schools by giving the actual score for the entire school district (Melendez & Konig, 2004).

Principals and similar school administrators realize the perceptions of measurable

school success are the results on standardized test scores. Parents and policymakers

already demonstrate a corporate, bottom-line mentality regarding test scores and appeals

to accountancy, both of which warp learning (Boyles, 2000). Teachers consistently are

subjected to the kind of corporate culture mentality common in business practice. Calls

for accountability, testing, and standardize curricula all point to business schemes and

corporate culture production. Schools assume the role of business, while administrators

become general managers, and teachers assume the role of workers. Students become the

result or product of knowledge in the business transaction.

Teachers are faced with corporate-culture expectations in their daily school lives

(Boyles, 2000), which is represented in schools by visionary charts, slogans, buttons, and

in-service day programs filled with overhead presentations about teamwork and systems

thinking. Teachers are subjected to the corporate concept of team-building games and

performances. The effort is technorationalistic in that it offers successful methods from

business and human resource consultants on how to influence the culture of the school.

Learning and achievement are purported to be easy to identify and quantify.

Learning and achievement can be accurately measured and reduced to numerical scores,

the basis upon which students, teachers, and schools will be judged as succeeding or

failing, and consequently rewarded or punished (Jackson, 2003).

According to the diagnosis and prescriptions of federal legislation including the

No Child Left Behind Act of 2001, the remedies for school improvement and the

achievement of excellence in student achievement and teachers' instruction appeal to

common sense, because results will be readily achievable through testing, testing, and more testing, complemented by a system of sanctions and rewards. This system has no room for inadequacy for students, teachers, and principals (Boyles, 2000).

The vast majority of Americans see testing as a useful way to ensure students are learning what is necessary for lifelong success (Finnermann, 2003). Discussions about testing lead to certain questions about the purpose of testing and the role of testing in public schools. Finnermann discussed the focus of testing as (a) whether or not the full range of desirable skills is thoroughly being assessed; (b) whether the standards of performance are fair and reasonable; (c) whether testing explains that the test is aligned with the curriculum; (d) whether school districts decide to consider test results in context with other indicators of student achievement; and (e) whether schools must consider test results as being properly interpreted and used for the purposes for which the tests were designed, and whether testing is being used for ultimate purpose to gain a better understanding of how well young people are learning and to gain insights into what can be done to enhance student learning. The use of standardized tests to gauge student learning and quantify educational practice leads to many questions about the proper use and reason for the use of standardized testing.

Schmoker (2000) explained that an emphasis on standardized tests does not have to be a lesson in "drill and kill" (p. 84). Research shows that students who attend schools creating an emphasis on subject matter, and students at schools where subject matter is made relevant and interesting are retaining more and will therefore earn higher scores on standardized tests. This finding indicates that these tests are useful, especially considering the evidence that an abundance of reading, writing, and authentic math experiences is possibly the best way to promote achievement on these tests. Standardized tests can reveal both progress and areas with the need for improvement. Without redirecting

alternative efforts to gauge student performance and higher order thinking skills,

standardized tests can help make comparative assessments on how well students are

learning basic knowledge and skills. Standardized achievement tests have been found to

be an impressive predictor of future student success, and the statistical reliability of

standardized tests is well documented (Leithwood et al., 2001). Standardized tests are

easy to administer, and if routinely used they provide a good first level of analysis

administrators wishing to improve school achievement (Schmoker, 2000).

Many schools, school districts, and state level departments of education use a

single measure for evaluating student progress employing conventional standardized,

norm- or criterion-referenced achievement tests (Senge et al., 2000). These tests,

including most state-level tests, only measure formal knowledge. Outcomes on these tests

arrive after months of delay and commonly after students have moved on to another

grade level. The results and information from the tests display only one or two highly

aggregated scores, giving students extremely limited information about academic

performance. Because the information is public knowledge, test scores are published in

newspapers, resulting in parents, real estate agents, politicians and other local

constituency having knowledge of school academic success.

The issue of the confusion between standardization and standards is of critical

importance, because increasingly scores of individual students' standardized tests of

academic skills and mastery of subject content carry serious consequences both for the

students and for those who teach the students (McNeil, 2000a). Decisions such as grade

placement and promotion or retention, placement in academic tracks, and even graduation increasingly are determined by students' scores on centrally imposed, commercially produced standardized tests. When tests are used in accountability systems, individual and aggregate student test scores are used as direct measures of teachers' work and production, the principal's performance, and overall school quality. These practices are highly questionable and are prompting serious scrutiny by policymakers and testing professionals on the possible misuses of student tests (McNeil, 2000a).

Ethical questions are being raised among testing experts regarding the use of standardized student tests for other purposes, including employee performance and school quality (McNeil, 2000a). These additional uses tend to be regarded by policymakers in heavily centralized states and districts as points requiring fine-tuning and are used as justification for extending tests to all grade levels and subjects, which will ensure consistency throughout a particular district or state. The final section of the literature reviews aspects of school leadership and the influence of standardized testing and school organizational culture.

Measuring student achievement via high-stakes testing may ignore the real progress of large percentages of students (Olson, 2005). Labels, according to the current system, recognize a student as proficient or non-proficient, which inadequately acknowledges progress made by the individual. Current data may be insufficient to accurately assess individual progress, because the system is built to rank and sort schools, classes, and groups. Norm-referenced testing and criterion-referenced testing may limit the rich experiences desired by students at any school level, because the focus of the curriculum is assessment based, compared to a curriculum that is experience based (Olson).

Wilson (2005) explained that the purpose of testing is to improve student learning and to provide a comprehensive description of student ability. Annual, summative testing procedures do not adequately portray the progress of students and the progress of the school as a learning community. Wilson concluded that school districts may wish to use a system of assessment implemented throughout the year, which acknowledges achievement, mastery, and progress supplementing the annual summative testing required by No Child Left Behind.

Creating a collaborative culture may be influential to student achievement (Akhavan, 2005). Although a great amount of work may be required to sustain a strong, performance-based culture, results that increase student achievement, according to standardized testing, may be worthwhile. According to Akhavan, changing the culture to incorporate experiences of success and failure communicated to the school staff will develop a rich, meaningful history from which to draw knowledge. Planning with clear goals and annual reflection allows the faculty to change the scope of instruction, thus leading to greater student involvement and possibly greater student achievement. Akhavan suggested that this focus transformed one particular California school from underperforming to high performing in 3 years.

School Leadership

Politicians and top educators are mindful of the perception placed on school systems regarding student achievement test outcomes (Boyles, 2000). Quantitative data and information recorded by testing are believed to lead to improved instructional practices. Similar to the business model of reviewing repeat customers, or observing product defects, data usage mirrors a corporate model (Glasser, 1998). Results and outcomes will not change unless instructional practices and the leadership guiding those practices change.

Valle (1999) explained that leadership in public organizations, including schools, must prepare organizational membership to cope, adapt, and change direction. This leadership will take increased energy from leaders and members. Standardized achievement testing has changed the paradigm of education from a supportive, culturally rich environment to a teleologically driven entity. Leaders unprepared for the changes placed on the position will not be able to lead the school organization effectively.

Integrity may be another term describing the behavior, which best leads to outstanding organizational performance (Badaracco & Ellsworth, 2004). Integrity suggests wholeness and coherence, rightness, and moral soundness. Aspects of leadership include personal values, beliefs, and assumptions. Leaders understand the impact of motivation and human behavior inside an organization, hold a strong set of personal ethics, and hold positive beliefs in the abilities of other organizational members. According to Badaracco and Ellsworth, integrity to hold a strong vision for the school organization, creating a strong collaborative culture based on community learning and measurable outcomes, describes the necessary paradigm for school leadership.

School administrators create effective change regarding school culture by modeling the values and beliefs important to the institution (Stolp, 1994). Principals acting with care and concern for others are more likely to develop a school culture with similar values. Another aspect important to leadership is shared vision. Shared vision is rooted in history, values, and beliefs (Stolp). Compatible individuals need to be hired reflecting the school's organizational culture and vision. Leaders need to do what is best for the organization (Stolp).

Leaders create change and redirect the culture of the organization toward improved measurable outcomes. Coleman (2004) described the situation in an urban, high-poverty community surrounded by public housing. Creating change involved changing the image and practices of the organization. First, the organization became a data-driven entity. Data were collected examining time management, engagement of students, and state assessments. The second change was the restoration of law and order. The school implemented strict guidelines regarding tardiness, absences, and instructional delivery. The school, and more importantly the principal, planned all activities together to ensure maximum educational delivery and standards-based instruction. The results from state-based assessments showed improvement from 14% to 57% across core subjects including mathematics and language arts. Writing assessment rose from 40% in 2001 to 100% in 2004 (Coleman). Leadership can redirect culture, as culture influences the outcomes of the organization.

School leaders understand school culture and the importance of standardized testing as the measure of school success (Lashway, 2001). The role of the school leader has changed from that of a manager or facilitator to instructional leader or lead teacher. This role places the leader in a position not only to manage items including bus schedules and difficult parents, but also to improve instructional delivery through modeling and practice. School leaders, traditionally, have not received the necessary training to fill the role of instructional leader (Lashway). Modern school leaders facilitate learning communities by fulfilling six roles, according to Lashway: (a) establishing student and adult learning as the main priority, (b) setting high expectations for performance, (c) having the leader direct content and instruction to standards, (d) creating a culture of continuous learning for adults, (e) reviewing and using multiple sources of data to assess learning, and (f) having the leader activate community support for school success (Lashway, 2001).

Holmes (2000) discussed three similar attributes of school leadership. School leaders need to understand the importance of instructional leadership, community leadership, and visionary leadership. The culture of the school leader, or principal, has shifted from the role of traditional manager to that of instructional leader basing decisions on student outcomes (Holmes, 2000). In some school districts, accountability for organizational achievement is tied to merit-based compensation measuring performance against expectations (Holmes, 2000).

Summary

Chapter 2 reviewed the related literature and research on school organizational culture, and standardized test scores as the measure of school success. The information presented serves as the conceptual framework for this study. The five sections of the literature review moved from the theories and components of organizational culture on to organizational, or corporate, culture and case studies researching the influence of culture on measurable outcomes, which reviewed aspects and effects of school organizational culture. The third section included case studies describing the influence of school organizational culture on educational outcomes, which included student achievement and school reform, leading to the fourth section explaining the role of standardized testing in modern education practice and the use of standardized testing as the measure of school success. The fifth and final section of the literature review described school leadership

and the focus of school leadership on school culture and standardized testing.

CHAPTER 3: METHODOLOGY

The purpose of this quantitative study was to discover the perceptions of school culture and correlate those perceptions with standardized test scores in elementary and secondary schools in southwestern Arizona. To examine this relationship, participating school districts and individual schools in southwestern Arizona were surveyed using the School Culture Survey (Leithwood et al., 2001). This survey examines aspects of school culture including the strength of relationships, forms of professional collaboration, climate of the physical environment, student-centered learning, and the professional work environment. The quantitative survey research method selected was appropriate to the study because the study quantified school organizational culture and student achievement test data. Once quantified, the results were correlated to discover if a relationship existed.

Research Method and Design Appropriateness

Quantitative methods, specifically the use of surveys, commonly are employed in education research (Smith & Glass, 1987). The quantitative approach uses strategies of inquiry such as experiments and surveys and collects statistical data on predetermined instruments (Creswell, 2003). As a method, the survey is a research tool in which a sample of subjects is drawn from a population and studied in order to make inferences about the population (Vogt, 1999). This design contrasts with the true experiment, in which subjects are assigned randomly to conditions or treatments. According to Vogt, surveys may measure abstract ideas within research, and in education may measure school culture, school leadership, student motivation, or teacher quality.

Quantitative research is deductive because it uses concepts, theories, and preconceived variables to determine what variables will be collected (Creswell, 2003).

Creswell (2003) described the typical deductive approach as (a) testing or verifying a theory, (b) testing of research questions or hypotheses, (c) defining or operationalizing variables derived from theory, and (d) measuring or observing variables using an instrument. In quantitative research, the social environment, culture, is represented by numerical data (Creswell, 2003). These data are analyzed statistically, and statistical inference procedures are used to generalize results obtained from samples to a referent population (Creswell, 2003). Quantitative methods are appropriate when ideas are generalized, behavior is consistent, and large samples are under study or deductive theory testing is the goal (Smircich, 1985).

The basis of quantitative research is derived from positivism, which claims knowledge is gained from the empirical study of natural or human phenomena and its properties and relations (Gall, Borg, & Gall, 1996; Vogt, 1999). Classical positivism suggests that social reality is viewed as a concrete structure of relationships between humans. The environment conditions humans to act in predictable manners and that acts are quantifiable. The neopositivist view is held by functionalists and concerns social reality as an evolving process of interaction and influence (Smircich, 1985). This reality does not clearly indicate causation in relationships, but rather influence in relationships. The classical approach indicates concrete ideas, compared to the functionalist approach suggesting influence over time (Smircich 1985; Vogt 1999).

Qualitative research differs from quantitative research regarding the study of organizational culture or school culture and measurable organizational outcomes, because qualitative research alone cannot reveal systematic comparisons. The study of culture, in qualitative terms, has its roots in cultural anthropology and American sociology. This process is an investigative process of describing and classifying social phenomena over extended periods. The researcher becomes a member of the world being studied and records information to describe perspective and meaning of members (Creswell, 2003; Hofstede, Neuijen, Ohayv, & Sanders, 1990). Marshall and Rossman (1999) suggested that qualitative research entails immersion in the everyday life of the setting chosen for the study; the researcher enters the informants' world and, through ongoing interaction, seeks the informants' perspectives and meanings. Qualitative design differs from quantitative design regarding the establishment of theories and hypotheses prior to the recording of data. Qualitative design expresses data in pictures, words, and written text, compared to the significance of numerical data in the quantitative comparison or correlation.

Qualitative design, regarding culture, reveals the concept of culture over time, describes the depth and richness of the information and social phenomena, and compares the change dynamics within the culture throughout observation. Schein (1990) criticized the study of culture through quantitative methods because this process does not reveal the richness or depth of an organization. Questionnaires or surveys are not designed to reveal the underlying knowledge within an organization. They are designed to measure values and norms, which have a direct influence on daily organizational operation; thus, the quantitative method was more useful for this study (Rollins & Roberts, 1998). The survey used for this study and the research questions of this study were designed to quantify school organizational culture by measuring specific items related to educational operation and ideology. The numerical data generated from this survey allowed for the analysis of relationships between school culture and standardized test score data.

As a method, the survey is a research tool in which a sample of subjects is drawn from a population and studied with the intention of making inferences to a larger population (Vogt, 1999). This design contrasts with the true experiment, in which subjects are assigned randomly to conditions or treatments. Vogt noted that surveys may measure abstract ideas within research, and in education may measure school organizational culture, school leadership, and so on.

The survey is often employed in the quantitative study of organizational culture. A study of organizational culture in corporations found 69 case studies where the primary instrument to collect data was the survey (Rollins & Roberts, 1998). The research involved exploring case studies of culture in the United States, Canada, and the United Kingdom. The study revealed that surveys are a popular tool in organizations and that different types of organizations are using surveys. These organizations include government, insurance, banking, health care, manufacturing, aerospace, technology, and office equipment.

Leithwood et al. (2001) described the following general guidelines about survey design:

1. Determine the goals and objectives.

2. Identify the variables.

3. Agree which indicators should be measured.

4. Draft the measures to reference the indicators.

5. Word the questions clearly and simply.

6. Ensure that the question or item addresses only one indicator.

7. Consider carefully the order in which you place the questions.

8. Pilot test the items.

9. Consider carefully the measurement scale.

Leithwood et al. further indicated that the reaction to surveys is usually one of the following: (a) accept them if they like the results, (b) attack the reliability and the validity if the results are disliked, and (c) begin to think about why the data state what they state.

Salient points of the descriptive survey include the following (Leedy & Ormond, 2001):

1. Descriptive survey methods deal with a situation that demands the technique of observation as the principle method of data collection.

2. The population of the study must be carefully chosen, clearly defined, and specifically delimited to set precise parameters for ensuring discreteness to the population.

3. Data in descriptive surveys are susceptible to distortion through bias. The researcher must be cautious when safeguarding the data from the influence of bias (Leedy & Ormond, 2001).

Traditionally, survey research in education has been a poorly executed task (M. Smith & Glass, 1987). Education researchers have used surveys to construct weak questionnaires and accepted any results therein without question. This was to complete the dissertation process, and the research frequently had no useable results for leadership (M. Smith & Glass). Rollins and Roberts (1998) explained that when organizations, and especially organizational leadership, desire change the use of surveys to record employee views are compared to "hard or objective" measures of performance (p. 85). The use of this method is relatable to a school as an organization and allows leadership to draw

conclusions about organizational performance.

Instruments

School Culture Survey

The survey used in this study was the School Culture Survey designed by

Leithwood and colleagues (2001). The survey instrument uses a Likert-type scale, which

is a widely used questionnaire format developed by Rensis Likert and frequently used in

survey research. The scale usually has five responses to a given question. Likert-type

scales are commonly used in education and social science research because of the high

reliability, easy construction, and useable format (Vogt, 1999).

The survey began by asking the participants their role as either a teacher or

principal. In the next section, participants indicated feelings about aspects of school

organizational culture using a 5-point Likert-type scale (1 = *strongly agree*, 2 = *agree*, 3

= *disagree*; 4 = *strongly disagree*; 5 = *NA* (nonapplicable or do not know). The survey

indicated seven areas of significance with regard to school culture:

1. The first area is strength, which deals with relationships, values and beliefs

throughout the organization.

2. Form is concerned with professional dialogue between teachers and staff.

3. Safe and orderly content concerns student behavior and the safety atmosphere

of the school facility.

4. Positivity is the smallest area, consisting of only two questions dealing with

student rewards and recognition of accomplishment.

5. Student-centered content the mission of the school as student centered.

57

6. Student learning questions ask about teacher feelings toward student learning and instructional delivery.

7. The final section of the survey discusses the professional work environment. Questions in this section regard staff development and implementation of new programs.

A mean score was tabulated for each school participating in the study. The closer the mean score was to 1.00, the higher the level of perceived school organizational culture.

This particular survey was chosen because it is relatively short compared to similar school culture surveys, and local school administrators typically do not want principals and teachers to spend a large amount of time participating in a study. Other reasons the survey was chosen include the scope of the questionnaire and the particular information asked of the participant, the ability of the instrument to measure organizational culture regardless of school size or location, and the reliability of the survey as explained by the authors. The reliability alpha of the School Culture Survey is listed by the authors at .917 (Leithwood et al., 2001). The alpha refers to a measure of internal reliability of the items being measured (Vogt, 1999).

A short demographic survey was included with the School Culture Survey. The survey participants indicated the following: (a) name of school where employed during the 2003–2004 school year, (b) gender, (c) age, (d) total years of teaching experience, (e) total years of administrative experience, (f) years of experience accumulated by the 2003–2004 school year, (g) grade taught during the 2003–2004 school year, and (h) race.

Stanford Achievement Test, Ninth Edition (SAT-9).

The SAT-9 is a standardized, norm-referenced test. The test assesses reading, mathematics, and language arts in a multiple-choice format. Three types of reading comprehension material are tested: (a) textural, or nonfiction and general information; (b) recreational, or fiction; and (c) functional, or material encountered in everyday life, such as advertisements. Test questions use various comprehension skills from the basic literal level up to the inferential and critical levels of reading comprehension (Arizona Department of Education, 2004).

The mathematics assessment explores the ability to compute as well as apply math concepts to problem-solving situations. Skills in interpreting a graph or a chart and in the application of principles of geometry, measurement and probability are also assessed (Arizona Department of Education, 2004).

The language arts portion of the SAT-9 assesses punctuation and capitalization skills and the ability to apply grammatical concepts correctly. Questions on the test also assess language expression, or the ability to manipulate words, phrases and clauses, and the ability to recognize correct, effective sentence structure, and writing style (Arizona Department of Education, 2004).

Scores on the SAT-9 are explained in score groupings called percentile ranks. These scores are divided by school, class, and individual students. Percentile ranks reflect a percentage compared to other schools, classes, or students taking the test. If a school score is 39, the average student at this school scored better than 39% of the students in the norming group. This study used school-wide scores for correlation with school culture means (Arizona Department of Education, 2004).

The reliability of the SAT-9 is estimated by alternate-forms reliability. This is a rigorous measure of test precision, taking into account differences arising from different testing situations and from different but equivalent test content. The reliability for total reading is 0.87, mathematics 0.88, and language 0.84 (Harcourt Assessment, Inc., 2004). The SAT-9 was used as the measure of student achievement because of its use throughout the United States and because it is not designed to measure achievement based upon a particular state-sanctioned curriculum. Arizona's Instrument to Measure Standards (AIMS), a criterion-referenced examination, was considered but not chosen because the exam is still in its infancy and has undergone revisions, making the results inconsistent for use in the research project.

Sound research practices suggest that questionnaires are easy to understand, create minimal confusion, and convey the proper idea (Rollins & Roberts, 1998) Questionnaires are tested for precision of expression, objectivity, relevance, suitability to the problem situation, and probability of favorable reception and return to maintain their veracity. Reliability of the instrument is the ability to produce consistent results, and time, convenience, and length of the questionnaire are considered in the design. Upon completion of the collection of data, the results must be organized and presented systematically so that valid and accurate conclusions can be drawn (Leedy & Ormond, 2001).

Document review in the research of education includes any number of school records. Schools generate a great amount of data that are compiled annually. Information may include student discipline, test scores, report cards, attendance, lunch counts, or sports participation. The availability to use this data may enhance research in a correlation study. According to Smith and Glass (1987), the use of data records should be evaluated according to source and purpose. Records act as an artifact in any organization and, if substantial and noteworthy, represent a picture of the organization.

The documents used for this study are the results of the 2004 SAT-9 (Harcourt Assessment, Inc., 2004). These results are available from the state of Arizona Department of Education and are public knowledge.

Population and Sampling

The population and sample of this study was comprised of all participating elementary and secondary school teachers and principals in the Yuma Elementary, Crane Elementary, Somerton Elementary, Wellton Elementary, Hyder Elementary, Mohawk Valley Elementary, Sentinel Elementary, Palo Verde Elementary, Antelope Union High School, and Yuma Union High School districts during the 2003-2004 school term. These school districts are located in the southwest corner of Arizona. The existing elementary and secondary schools in Yuma County and two elementary schools bordering Yuma County were solicited to participate in the study. Overall, 17 of 35 possible schools, 5 years or older, agreed to participate in the study. Teachers, including resident speech therapists, school psychologists, and other related personnel; principals; and assistant principals were invited to participate in the study.

Data Collection

The data for this study were collected from surveys completed by teachers and principals in participating schools as well as SAT-9 achievement test data from the Arizona Department of Education. Local school district superintendents were asked to participate in the research study. The researcher used the Informed Consent: Permission to Use Premises document from the University of Phoenix (2002) *Research Handbook* to ask approval to survey principals and teachers at each school site within the given school district. The sample was created from these written permissions and participating schools' teachers and principals. The informed consent explained that permission from the superintendent includes each school site within the school district, however, it is understood that some principals may not wish to participate in the study. Copies of the permission forms are located in Appendix B. Permission to reproduce the survey is available in Appendix C, and a copy of the survey is available in Appendix D.

Upon receiving Institutional Review Board approval, a packet was distributed to each participating school site principal including (a) a letter introducing the researcher and the nature of the research, (b) copies of the School Culture Survey, (c) copies of the demographic survey (Appendix E), and (d) an envelope to collect the data. Copy amounts were contingent on the number of teachers and principals. The researcher allowed the necessary time for the principal to distribute the survey and demographic questionnaire to all teachers in the school. Upon completing the survey and demographic data, the researcher collected the packet at the school site. Schools located a considerable distance from the researcher received a prepaid envelope to mail the packet.

SAT-9 data in the form of test scores for the 2003–2004 school year were collected from the Arizona Department of Education (2004) Web site for each participating school. Standardized test scores are made public by the Arizona Department of Education and local school districts via publication in newspapers, mailings to parents, and district Web sites. Results represented the 2003–2004 school year and reflected scores for mathematics, language, and reading. Completed surveys, demographic data, and SAT-9 data were placed in an envelope to ensure that information reflected only the participating schools and that data were not crossed with any other school. Each school received a number designation so that data could be disseminated easily and schools would not be recognized. The SAT-9 scores for the study comprised Grades 2–12, depending on particular grades in each school, as some schools were elementary and others secondary. Grade participation per school was not described because that information would allow the reader to distinguish SAT-9 scores and school culture scores of participating schools and could compromise the anonymity of participants. The scores were compiled to reach a mean score. A letter regarding the use of the SAT-9 is available in Appendix F.

Data collected from the School Culture Survey were divided by school and calculated to a mean score. The scores on this survey range from 5.00 to 1.00, with 1.00 being the highest possible score. Achievement test score data from the SAT-9 were collected and quantified by school site. Each participating school in the study had scores in mathematics, language, and reading for each grade. These scores were averaged, creating a mean score for a participating school in each subject area. The mean scores in each subject area were averaged so that each school had a mean SAT-9 score. SAT-9 scores are based on percentile ranks, and a score of 39, for example, concludes that all students in the school score better than 39% of all students participating in the test in the norming group.

Each school is represented by a mean culture score, by mean SAT-9 scores in mathematics, language, reading, and by a total mean score for all subjects. These data were used by the researcher for the purpose of correlation between school organizational culture and standardized test scores.

Validity

The validity of the School Culture Survey was determined by consultation with school district superintendents in southwestern Arizona. Participating superintendents and principals noted the overall length of the survey and the survey's detail regarding the focus on students.

Vogt (1999) defined *validity* as "a term to describe a measurement instrument or test that accurately measures what it is supposed to measure; the extent to which a measure is free of system error" (p. 301). According to Creswell (2003), researchers need to understand threats to validity as internal and external. Internal validity threats are treatments or experiences of the participants that threaten the researcher's ability to draw correct inferences from the data. Participants in a survey instrument may change during the questionnaire, misunderstand the system of the survey, or be dishonest from fear of retribution. External validity threats are summarized as the research draws inferences to data from other samples and settings. For instance, it is incorrect to believe that the data in an education based research project are applicable to a health care setting (Creswell, 2003).

Data Analysis

Descriptive research describes existing phenomena. Descriptive research commonly uses descriptive statistics. Descriptive statistics are procedures for organizing, graphing, summarizing, and describing quantitative information (Smith & Glass, 1987; Vogt, 1999). Descriptive research tests hypotheses or answers questions based on the data collected by the researcher. Educational research is inclined to discover causation or change; the purpose of this study was to discover if relationships exist between variables, making descriptive research appropriate (Gall et al., 1996; Rollins & Roberts, 1998).

Correlation research attempts to determine whether, and to what extent, a relationship exists between two or more quantifiable variables (Vogt, 1999). Smith and Glass (1987) explained that correlation studies serve two purposes:

> The first is building theory about phenomenon by better understanding the constructs, what they consist of, and how they relate to other constructs. The second purpose is to enable researchers to predict one variable from another (or several others). If two variables correlate with each other and the researcher knows an individual's status on one of them, then that person's status on the second variable can be forecast or predicted. (pp. 198–199)

Correlation does not always imply causation (Creswell, 2003). Errors in correlation studies point to causation when variables are not clearly defined. A *lurking variable* affects the variables but is not included in the study. In education research, lurking variables may be damaging to research. Research on school lunch programs may indicate that students are wealthy enough not to purchase school lunches; however, the students may think the food has a bad taste. Lurking variables in education include teacher quality and experience, poverty and wealth, parent education and support, and government intervention and finances (Smith & Glass, 1987; Triola, 2001).

Correlation studies commonly use a survey and document review to obtain data (Smith & Glass, 1987). Surveys and document reviews may serve as variables in a correlation, because a correlation can compare the results of a survey against document review data (Smith & Glass). This research design was most appropriate for this study because it could (a) quantify school organizational culture, (b) reveal school success via the collection of standardized test score data, and (c) allow the researcher to draw conclusions regarding the relationship between said variables.

Organization and Clarity

By surveying schools to determine organizational culture, the researcher was able to recognize the perceived school organizational culture of each participating school. This method allowed the researcher to quantify the results of the survey and to use the data for subsequent correlation with hard data. These hard data were represented by the standardized test scores of participating schools.

Summary

The purpose of chapter 3 was to describe the methodology that was used to collect data from participating schools regarding school organizational culture and to correlate the data with standardized test scores. The quantitative approach to this study allowed for the quantifying of school organizational culture and standardized test scores. This quantification allowed the researcher to correlate the variables regarding each research question. A step-by-step discussion of the design allowed for replication at a later date by other researchers. Chapter 4 will continue by analyzing the data and presenting the findings. Chapter 5 will complete the study with implications of the research, conclusions, and recommendations for further study.

CHAPTER 4: PRESENTATION AND ANALYSIS OF DATA

This chapter details the presentation of the data analysis of the study presented in the previous chapters. The chapter begins with a statement of the problem and discussion of the population and survey instruments, advances to a discussion of results relevant to each research question, and culminates with a summary.

The purpose of this quantitative study was to discover the perceptions of school culture and correlate those perceptions with standardized test scores in elementary and secondary schools in southwestern Arizona. Standardized test scores provide an approach to measuring school success similar to accounting practices used in business demonstrating a corporate mentality, production-line oriented process (Boyles, 2000). Empirical evidence suggests that organizational culture influences measurable business outcomes; additionally, researchers (Craig et al., 2005; Reavis et al., 1999) have reported that a focus on school culture has increased student outcomes and that positive school culture is a common characteristic of high-performing schools. However, research on the concept of school culture and culture's influence on measurable school outcomes is limited (Collins, 2004; Collins & Porras, 1997; Deal & Kennedy, 1982; Detert, 2000; Hall & Hord, 2001; Heskett & Kotter, 1992; Schein, 1992).

The existing situation is that school leaders measure success as student achievement through performance on standardized tests and expect outcomes that are quantifiable, much like business leaders use quantitative data to measure business success (Boyles, 2000). Although it is the current paradigm of achievement, standardized testing is essentially a snapshot of student ability, which may fail to recognize the essence of student potential, growth, or achievement in all subjects (Boyles, 2000; Olson, 2005;

Wilson, 2005). Additionally, although student achievement is measured by standardized test scores, it is influenced by school culture (Stolp & Smith, 1995). While business success is often quantifiable by dollar returns on products, and thus can be quantified without factoring in the business culture, the product of schools is the achievement of its human capital, students. The human capital or students are affected by the culture in which they are expected to achieve. This study was designed to be similar to studies by Heskett and Kotter (1992), Collins and Porras (1997), and Kotter et al. (1997) measuring organizational culture to outcomes (Rollins & Roberts, 1998). This quantitative correlation study was designed to determine whether perceived school culture related to student achievement as measured by standardized test scores in a population of 17 elementary and secondary schools located in southwestern Arizona.

Description of Population Data and Survey

The population and sample of this study was comprised of all participating elementary and secondary school teachers and principals in the Yuma Elementary, Crane Elementary, Somerton Elementary, Wellton Elementary, Hyder Elementary, Mohawk Valley Elementary, Sentinel Elementary, Palo Verde Elementary, Antelope Union High School, and Yuma Union High School districts during the 2003–2004 school term. These school districts are located in the southwest corner of Arizona (see Appendix G for a description of the region). A total of 369 individual surveys were returned representing 17 schools. Some of the returned surveys were not used in the data analysis for the study due to a limited number of years of service at that particular school, and it was decided by the researcher that a minimum of 5 years of service would be sufficient to gauge cultural knowledge, as 5–8 years is accepted as mastery in the teaching profession (Scherer,

2001). Years of experience data were gathered with a demographic survey that was included with the School Culture Survey sent to participating schools. Table 1 covers study participation.

Table 1

Study Participation

School	Participants with 5 years or more experience	Total survey	Percentage
1	11	19	58%
2	8	14	57%
3	4	14	29%
4	5	41	12%
5	12	12	100%
6	9	22	41%
7	8	21	38%
8	7	45	16%
9	3	8	38%
10	14	14	100%
11	18	18	100%
12	10	23	43%
13	6	6	100%
14	6	28	21%
15	4	11	36%
16	8	12	67%
17	12	61	20%
Total	145	369	

The School Culture Survey designed by Leithwood and colleagues (2001) was used for this study. The survey indicates the following seven areas of significance with regard to school culture:

1. Strength deals with relationships, values, and beliefs throughout the organization. The surveyor asks the respondent to consider the strength of similar values, beliefs, and attitudes between teachers and administrators. The relationships between colleagues, students and staff, and working departments complete the first segment of the survey.

2. Form is concerned with professional dialogue between teachers and staff. Questions in this section include sharing and conversing regarding professional teaching practices and observations.

3. The section entitled Content is Safe and Orderly concerns student behavior and the safety atmosphere of the school facility. The respondent is asked to consider the overall physical safety and disciplinary procedures of the surveyed school.

4. Content is Positive explores positive school content. This is the shortest area of the survey, consisting of only two questions dealing with student rewards and recognition of accomplishment.

5. Content is Student Centered discusses the mission of the school as student centered. The section contains six questions regarding the expectations of students and the student–teacher relationship.

6. Content Fosters Learning for Students includes four questions concerning student leaning. The researcher asks the teacher about feelings toward student learning and instructional delivery.

7. The final section, Content is Designed to Provide a Professional Work Environment for Staff, discusses the professional work environment in seven questions. Questions in this section regard staff development and implementation of new programs.

Description of the SAT-9

The SAT-9 is a standardized, norm-referenced test. The test is structured to assess reading, mathematics, and language arts in a multiple-choice format. Three types of reading comprehension material are tested: (a) textural, or nonfiction and general information; (b) recreational, or fiction; and (c) functional, or material encountered in everyday life, such as advertisements. Test questions employ various comprehension skills from the basic literal level up to the inferential and critical levels of reading comprehension (Arizona Department of Education, 2004).

The mathematics assessment explores the ability to compute as well as apply math concepts to problem-solving situations. Skills in interpreting a graph or a chart and in the application of principles of geometry, measurement and probability are also assessed (Arizona Department of Education, 2004). The reading section of the SAT-9 examines the ability of the student to comprehend reading passages, understand phonics and word recognition, and understand passages for general reading and instructional reading. The language arts portion of the SAT-9 assesses punctuation and capitalization skills and the ability to apply grammatical concepts correctly. Questions on the test also assess language expression, or the ability to manipulate words, phrases, and clauses, and the ability to recognize correct, effective sentence structure and writing style.

Scores on the SAT-9 are explained in percentile ranks. Percentile ranks reflect a percentage compared to other schools, classes or students taking the test. A school percentile rank of 39 means that the average student at this school scored better than 39% of the students in the norm group. This study used school-wide scores for correlation with school culture means (Arizona Department of Education, 2004).

The reliability of the SAT-9 is estimated by alternate-forms reliability. This is a rigorous measure of test precision, taking into account differences arising from different testing situations and from different but equivalent test content. The reliability for total reading is 0.87, mathematics 0.88, and language 0.84 (Harcourt Assessment, Inc., 2004).

The following is a discussion of the research questions for the study. The author presents each research question with corresponding tables and figures explaining the results of the data. The first research question presents the mean culture score for each participating school. The mean culture score was tabulated from the returned surveys used for the study. The second question presents the results of the SAT-9 for each participating school. The table displays the results for each subject area and an overall mean score for each participating school. Data were obtained through the Arizona Department of Education. The third question correlates the results of the mean school culture scores and the overall means for the SAT-9 achievement test.

Research Question 1

Research Question 1 was the following: What are the mean culture scores measured by the School Culture Survey for participating schools? Table 2 presents the mean culture scores derived from the School Culture Survey (Leithwood et al., 2001) for participating schools in the study. Each returned survey was organized by school and analyzed by each question on the questionnaire. Table 3 presents the data regarding both teacher perceptions of school culture and participating administrators' perceptions of school culture. The standard deviation represents the difference between teacher mean

culture scores and administrator mean culture scores.

Table 2

School Culture Survey Mean Scores and Standard Deviation

School	Mean	Standard deviation
School 1	1.41	0.30
School 2	1.46	0.36
School 3	1.61	0.31
School 4	1.65	0.38
School 5	1.65	0.42
School 6	1.68	0.38
School 7	1.67	0.39
School 8	1.68	0.58
School 9	1.77	0.45
School 10	1.75	0.42
School 11	1.79	0.48
School 12	1.79	0.33
School 13	1.99	0.48
School 14	2.05	0.39
School 15	2.19	0.82
School 16	2.28	0.54
School 17	2.33	0.51

Table 3

Teacher and Administrator Mean Culture Scores

School	Teacher mean culture score	Administrator mean culture score	Standard deviation
School 1	1.24	1.60	0.25
School 2	1.46	1.46	0.00
School 3	1.77	1.68	0.06
School 4	1.63	1.76	0.09
School 5	1.7	1.58	0.08
School 6	1.67	1.68	0.01
School 7	1.66	1.78	0.08
School 8	1.79	1.32	0.34
School 9	1.73	2.10	0.26
School 10	1.80	1.32	0.34
School 11	1.79	1.79	0.00
School 12	1.82	1.61	0.15
School 13	1.93	2.44	0.36
School 14	2.04	2.13	0.06
School 15	2.24	2.38	0.09
School 16	2.26	2.38	0.08
School 17	1.96	2.38	0.30
Total	1.80	1.85	0.04

Mean scores and standard deviations on the School Culture Survey were calculated for each school. The Likert-type scale used in this survey is scored as follows: 1 = *strongly agree*, 2 = *agree*, 3 = *disagree*, 4 = *strongly disagree*, 5 = *NA* (*not applicable* or *do not know*). A mean score near 1.0 suggests that the culture of the school is an open atmosphere and has strong communication and collegial relationships among staff and administration. A mean score of approximately 4.0 suggests low communication; a rigid managerial style; and an unstable, unsafe atmosphere.

Research Question 2

Research Question 2 asked the following: What are the mean standardized test scores in language arts, reading, and mathematics as measured by the SAT-9 for participating schools? Table 4 presents the mean SAT-9 test scores in language arts, reading, and mathematics for participating schools in the 2003–2004 school term. The scores are the means for each subject area and the overall mean to create a composite mean score. The scores were provided by the Arizona Department of Education (2004).

Research Question 3

Research Question 3 asked the following: Is there a relationship between school organizational culture as measured by the School Culture Survey and the results of standardized test scores in language arts, reading, and mathematics as measured by the SAT-9? For Research Question 3, the mean school culture scores and the mean SAT-9 results were correlated to discover if any relationship existed between perceived school culture and measurable student achievement. A standard statistics program was used for the correlation to generate results, and those results were used to build the charts for

Figures 1–6. Tables 5 and 6 present a comparison of mean culture scores and mean SAT-9 results for participating schools. Figures 1–5 chart the results of the correlation.

Table 4

Subject Scores and Percentile Ranks for the Stanford Achievement Test, Ninth Edition

School	Math	Reading	Language arts	Rounded percentile rank
School 1	74.0	63.8	59.6	65.8
School 5	69.0	56.5	62.0	62.5
School 15	65.3	51.6	48.4	55.1
School 8	52.8	56.0	54.6	54.5
School 3	64.2	47.0	50.6	53.9
School 6	61.2	53.5	43.8	52.8
School 7	58.7	48.9	50.6	52.7
School 10	49.0	46.0	51.3	48.8
School 2	44.8	40.5	55.0	46.8
School 4	50.0	42.0	43.0	45.0
School 13	52.5	42.0	39.0	44.5
School 12	52.1	39.4	35.3	42.3
School 17	50.0	41.0	33.0	41.3
School 14	50.0	35.0	33.0	39.3
School 11	57.0	27.0	32.0	38.7
School 16	48.0	28.0	27.0	34.3
School 9	35.0	33.0	31.0	33.0

Table 5

Ranking of Schools by Highest Mean School Culture Score With Mean Stanford

Achievement Test, Ninth Edition, Percentile Rank

School	Mean culture score	Stanford Achievement Test, Ninth Edition, percentile rank mean
School 1	1.41	65.80
School 2	1.46	46.75
School 3	1.61	53.93
School 4	1.65	45.00
School 5	1.65	62.50
School 6	1.68	52.83
School 7	1.67	52.73
School 8	1.68	54.46
School 9	1.77	33.00
School 10	1.75	48.77
School 11	1.79	38.67
School 12	1.79	42.26
School 13	1.99	44.50
School 14	2.05	39.33
School 15	2.19	55.10
School 16	2.28	34.33
School 17	2.33	41.33

Table 5 presents the data by mean culture score with the corresponding SAT-9

test results in the column to the right. The schools are in order from highest mean culture score to lowest mean culture score. The top 8 schools in the study show that 6 schools scored above the 50th percentile rank on the SAT-9 test, compared to the bottom 9 schools, where only 1 school scored above the 50th percentile rank.

Table 6 ranks schools in ascending order by mean SAT-9 results with the corresponding mean culture score in the column to the right. School 1 had the highest mean SAT-9 score and the highest mean school culture score. School 5 had a high mean SAT-9 score and a relatively high mean culture score compared to other participating schools. School 15 is an anomaly, having a high mean SAT-9 score and a relatively low mean school culture score. The data suggest a trend between the top 9 schools having a mean culture score near 1.5 and the higher SAT-9 achievement scores. Figures 1 and 2 display the data in two separate charts providing the correlation results. The results of the correlation concluded the populations were correlated with a correlation coefficient, $r = -.52, p < .05$.

Table 6

Ranking of Schools from Lowest to Highest Mean Stanford Achievement Test, Ninth

Edition, Percentile Rank With Corresponding Mean School Culture Survey Score

School	Stanford Achievement Test, Ninth Edition, percentile rank mean	Mean culture score
School 9	33.00	1.77
School 16	34.33	2.28
School 11	38.67	1.79
School 14	39.33	2.05
School 17	41.33	2.33
School 12	42.26	1.79
School 13	44.50	1.99
School 4	45.00	1.65
School 2	46.75	1.46
School 10	48.77	1.75
School 7	52.73	1.67
School 6	52.83	1.68
School 3	53.93	1.61
School 8	54.46	1.68
School 15	55.10	2.19
School 5	62.50	1.65
School 1	65.80	1.41

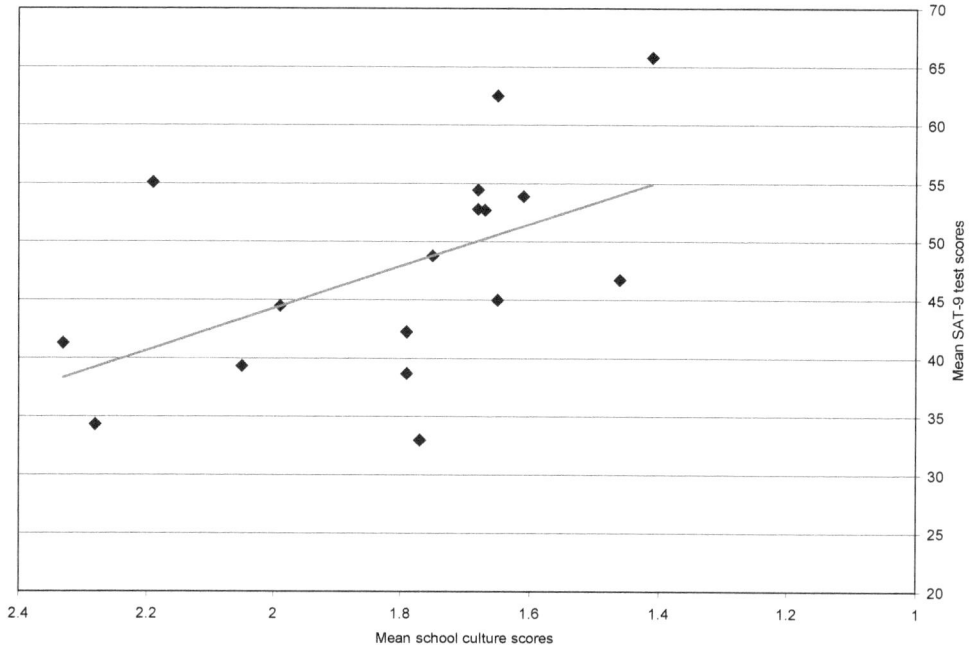

Figure 1. Correlation between mean school culture scores and mean Stanford

Achievement Test, Ninth Edition, percentile rank scores.

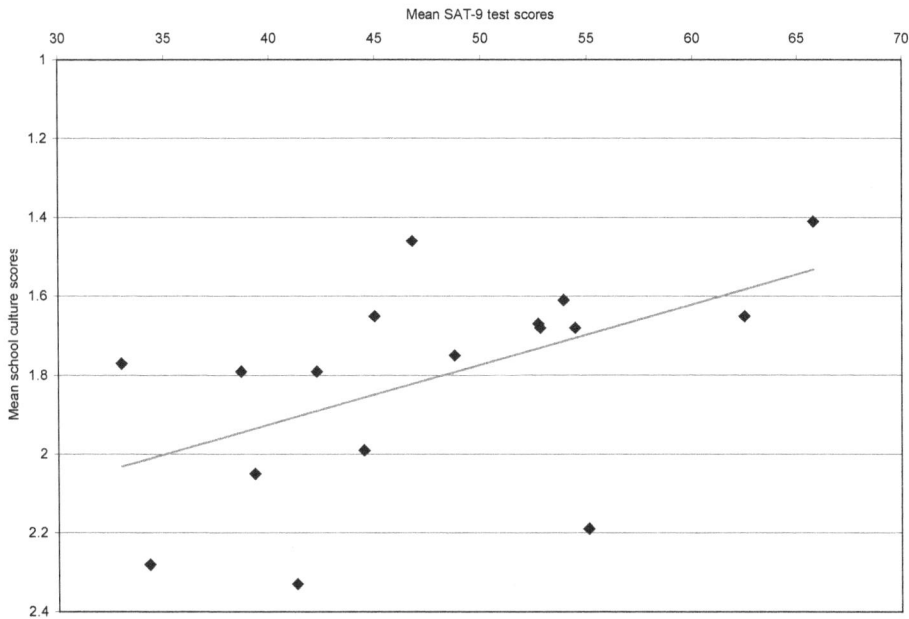

Figure 2. Correlation between mean school culture survey scores and mean Stanford Achievement Test, Ninth Edition, percentile rank scores.

Figures 3, 4, and 5 present the mean culture scores for participating schools correlated with SAT-9 mean scores for each subject area, including mathematics, reading, and language arts. Figure 3 presents SAT-9 mean scores in mathematics correlated with mean culture scores; results indicated the two populations were not correlated with the correlation coefficient, $r = -.28$, $p < .05$.

The data regarding mean SAT-9 reading scores presented similar findings, displayed in Figure 4. The results for the correlation between mean culture scores and SAT-9 mean reading scores showed that the populations were not correlated with a correlation coefficient, $r = -.48$, $p < .05$.

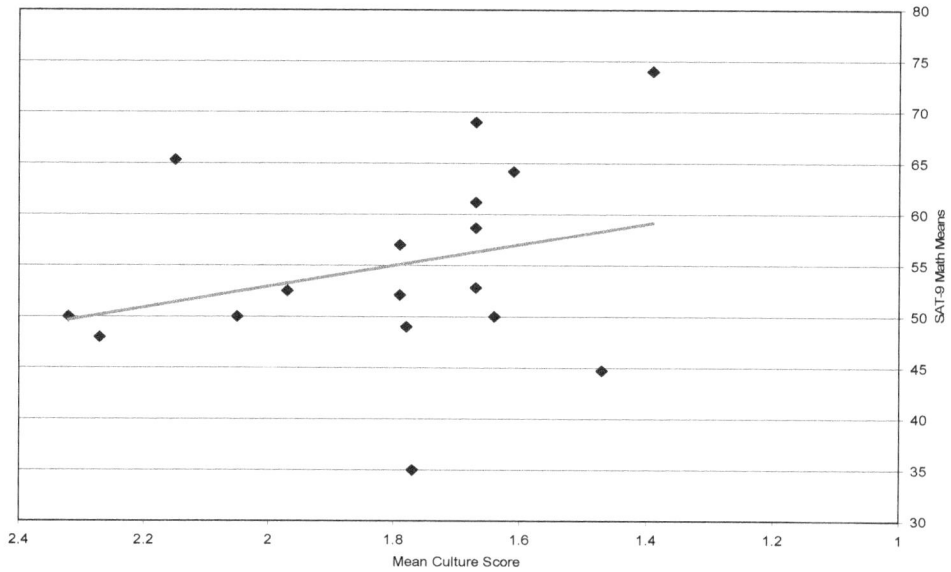

Figure 3. Correlation between mean school culture survey scores and mean Stanford

Achievement Test, Ninth Edition, math scores.

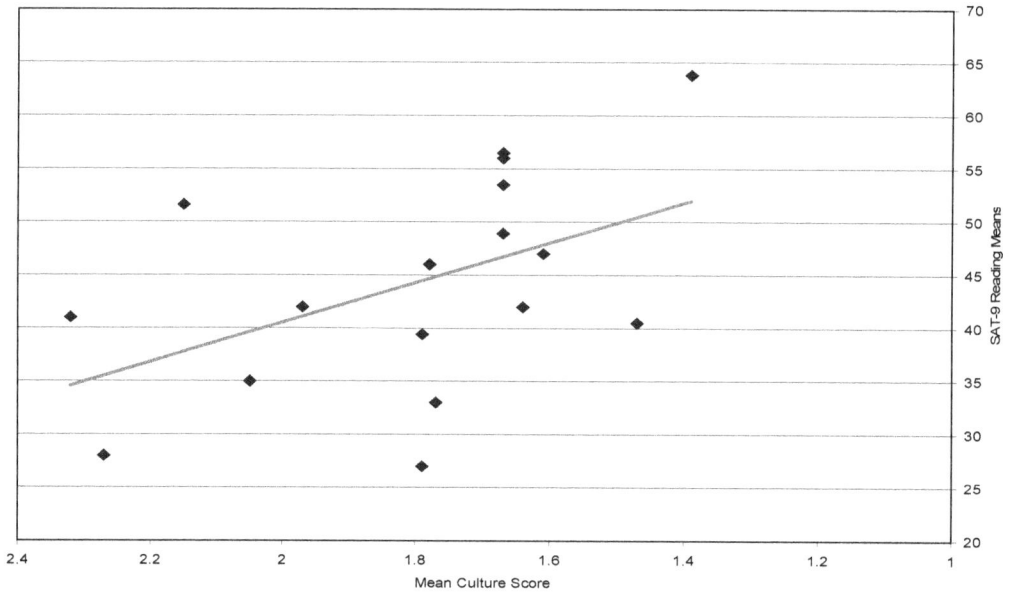

Figure 4. Correlation between mean school culture survey scores and mean Stanford

Achievement Test, Ninth Edition, reading scores.

Figure 5 presents the correlation between mean culture scores and SAT-9 mean language arts scores. Analysis of the data concluded that the populations were correlated with a correlation coefficient, $r = -.67$, $p < .05$.

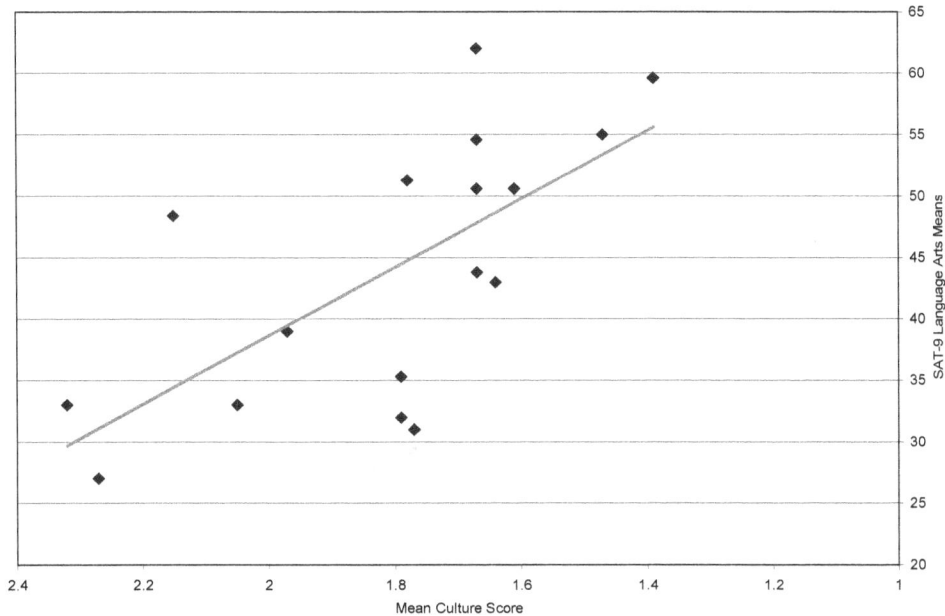

Figure 5. Correlation between mean school culture survey scores and mean Stanford Achievement Test, Ninth Edition, language arts scores.

Figure 6 presents information for participating teachers with 5 or more years of experience along with mean school culture scores. The data suggest that participation of teachers with more experience had no relationship with mean culture scores. The mean culture scores showed a steady rise in scores from School 1 through School 17 compared with the percentage of teachers with 5 years of experience, which varied between participating schools. Table 3 displays these data as well.

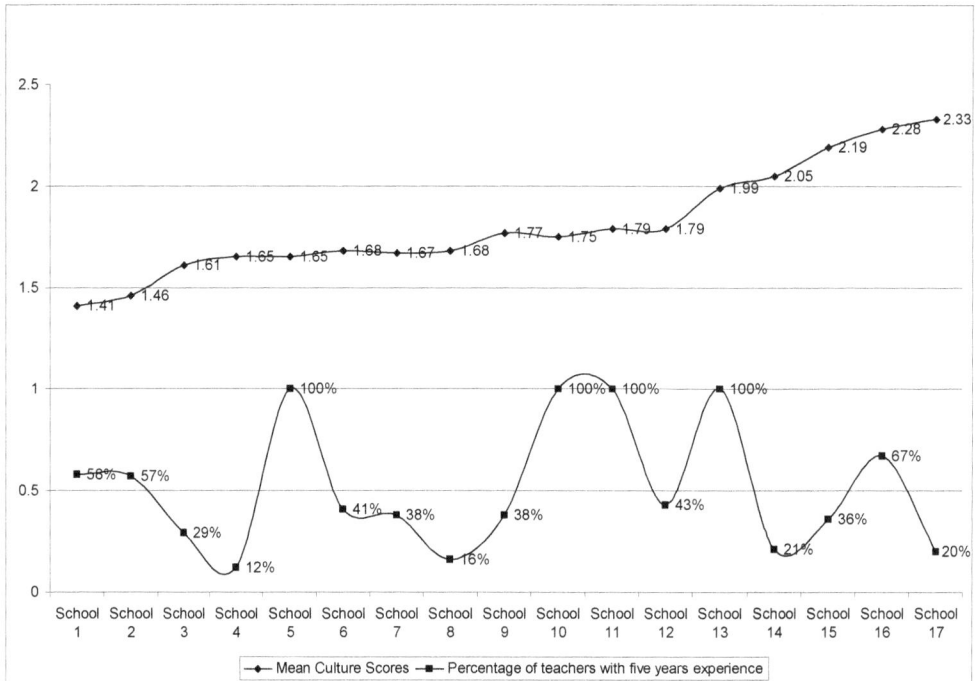

Figure 6. Percentage of teachers with 5 years of experience and mean school culture scores.

Summary

Chapter 4 presented the data compiled from the School Culture Survey (Leithwood et al., 2001), SAT-9 scores, and the correlated information from both instruments. Survey results were calculated into a mean score and presented for each participating school. SAT-9 test results were presented for each school, including mean scores in the subjects of reading, language arts, and mathematics and an overall mean score representing a basic idea of conclusive student achievement. Chapter 5 summarizes the study findings and provides recommendations, future research possibilities, and conclusions for the field of education leadership.

CHAPTER 5: SUMMARY AND RECOMMENDATIONS

Chapter 5 provides a summary and discussion of the findings of the study with conclusions from each research question, implications for the field of education leadership, and recommendations for further research. The research project derived from the lack of literature relating to understanding the influence of school culture on measurable school success. Although the study of school culture is not a new phenomenon and has been explored by various authors, empirical research correlating the results of student achievement and school culture is limited (Deal & Peterson, 1999b).

Standardized test scores provide an approach to measuring school success similar to accounting practices used in business demonstrating a corporate mentality and production-line oriented process (Boyles, 2000). Although empirical evidence suggests that organizational culture influences measurable business outcomes, research on the concept of school culture and culture's influence on measurable school outcomes is limited (Collins, 2004; Collins & Porras, 1997; Deal & Kennedy, 1982; Detert, 2000; Hall & Hord, 2001; Heskett & Kotter, 1992; Schein, 1992).

The existing situation is that school leaders measure success as student achievement through performance on standardized tests and expect quantifiable outcomes, much like business leaders use quantitative data to measure business success (Boyles, 2000). Although it is the current paradigm of achievement, standardized testing is essentially a snapshot of student ability, which may fail to recognize adequately the essence of student potential, growth, or achievement in all academic subjects (Boyles, 2000; Olson, 2005; Wilson, 2005). Although standardized test scores measure student achievement, student achievement is influenced by school culture (Stolp & Smith, 1995).

While business success is often quantifiable by dollar returns on products, and can be quantified without factoring in the business culture, the product of schools is the achievement of its human capital, students (Boyles, 2000). Failure to study school culture as influential to student outcomes may limit academic growth and may have serious consequences to overall school success as measured by testing. According to current research, cultural aspects of the school community should be considered in curriculum development, social initiatives, long-term academic planning, and student enrollment and screening procedures (Peterson, 2002). Lack of acknowledgement in these specific areas may allow culture to emerge without control; hence the school leadership and administration may be helpless to observe culture rather than direct culture. Without directing culture, administrators may be unable to guide the academic practices of the school thus influencing student achievement and success at every school level. School administrators in several schools, along with other researchers (Craig et al., 2005; Reavis, Vinson, & Fox, 1999) have reported that a focus on culture has increased student outcomes greatly and that culture is a common characteristic of high-performing schools. This study was designed to be similar to studies by Heskett and Kotter (1992); Collins and Porras (1997); and Kotter, Sasser, and Schlesinger (1997) measuring organizational culture to outcomes (Rollins & Roberts, 1998). This quantitative correlation study was designed to determine whether perceived school culture related to student achievement as measured by standardized test scores in a population of 17 elementary and secondary schools located in southwestern Arizona.

Summary and Discussion of Findings

The review and discussion of the findings summarizes the results of each research question and discusses the hypothesis. This discussion is followed by conclusions of the research collectively.

Research Question 1

What were the mean culture scores measured by the School Culture Survey for participating schools? Each survey received from participating schools was calculated to a mean score with the standard deviation calculated additionally. Results are displayed in Table 2. Participating schools were not divided into any subcategory as it was the desire of the researcher to explain the results without bias. No significant difference in school culture scores was evident due to school size or location. Preferably, scores for participating schools should be near a score of 1.0, indicating a strong, professional culture; all participating schools scored between 1.0 and 2.4. Results were tabulated by generating a mean score from each survey and the corresponding 38 questions, for each school. Additionally, results for teachers and administrators were tabulated and displayed in Table 3. Other data compiled included a demographic survey, which yielded information regarding teacher experience at each participating school, displayed in Table 1 and Figure 6.

Analysis of the results concluded that most participants in the study found their particular school to be adequate in all areas of the survey. Generally, school culture scores were on the high end of the Likert-type scale, falling between the range of 1.4 and 2.4. Considering the scale reaches to a score of 4, the overall perception from participants was that their school setting is an agreeable environment in which to work and learn.

Differences in mean culture scores between administrators and teachers suggest differences in cultural perception For example, in Schools 3, 5, 8, 10, and 12, perceptions of the cultural environment were perceived as better by administrators than by teachers. Of these schools, Schools 3, 5, 8, and 10 were in the top half of schools, as classified according to SAT-9 results. Only School 12 was not in the top half. These data suggest that the administrative view of school culture, and the administrative mode of operation may be most effective toward student achievement. The administrative cultural perception may be more accurate or generally more influential in the overall success and direction of the school staff and students. Schools 2 and 11 averaged the same score for teachers and administrators. School 6 had teachers scoring .01 more in perceptions of culture over administrators' perceptions of culture. There was no significance to SAT-9 for these particular schools. Schools 1, 4, 7, 9, 13, 14, 15, 16, and 17 displayed higher mean scores of teacher perceptions of culture compared to administrator perceptions of culture. Of these schools, Schools 1, 7, and 15 were in the top half of schools, as classified according to SAT-9 scores. Schools 4, 9, 13, 14, 16, and 17 were in the lower half of schools, according to SAT-9 results. Overall, 80% of schools with higher administrator perceptions of culture compared to teacher perceptions fared better on the SAT-9, compared to 33% of schools with higher teacher perceptions compared to administrator perceptions. The studies researched for the literature review of this dissertation did not record nor reveal similar data; rather, the studies focused on overall cultural perceptions and the influence of those perceptions on achievement.

Study participation did not seem to have an influence on mean school culture scores represented in Figure 6. Four participating schools (Schools 5, 10, 11, and 13) had

100% participation in the study, considering the requirement of teacher experience. Only School 5 was in the top half of mean culture scores and mean SAT-9 scores. School 10 fell near the center on both mean culture scores and mean SAT-9 scores. Schools 11 and 13 were in the lower half of the study in both mean culture scores and SAT-9 scores. The next group of schools, including Schools 16, 1, 2, 12, and 6, averaged participation between 41% and 67%. School 1, having the highest mean school culture score and SAT-9 score, ranked sixth in participation. Schools 2, 12, and 6 were near the center of the study regarding SAT-9 scores. School 16 ranked 5th in participation but was 16th in both SAT-9 and mean culture scores. Two schools recorded 38% participation. School 7 was near the center in both mean culture score and SAT-9 score. School 9 was near the center in mean culture score but ranked lowest in SAT-9 scores. Schools 3, 4, 8, 14, 15, and 17 were in the lower group of schools regarding participation of teachers with 5 years of experience. Schools 3 and 15 scored 29% and 36%, respectively, considering teacher participation. Both schools were divided greatly in mean culture score, with scores of 1.65 and 2.19, respectively. Schools 14 and 17 were near each other in teacher participation, scoring 20% and 2%, respectively. Both schools had similar SAT-9 scores, with scores of 39.33 and 41.33, respectively. Schools 8 and 4 had the lowest participation, with scores of 16% and 12%, respectively. Both schools were in the top 10 of SAT-9 scores and mean culture scores. School 8 was significantly higher in SAT-9 scores compared to other schools with low participation scores. These data suggest that greater or lesser participation in the study did not influence results.

Research Question 2

What were the mean standardized test scores in language arts, reading, and mathematics as measured by the SAT-9 for participating schools? Mean SAT-9 scores for participating schools indicated achievement in language arts, reading, and mathematics. The scores were averaged to an overall mean score. No significant difference in scores was evident due to school size or location.

School 1 scored the highest mean SAT-9 score and the highest mean school culture score. School 5 scored a high mean SAT-9 score and a relatively high mean culture score compared to other participating schools. School 15 is an anomaly, having a high mean SAT-9 score and a relatively low mean school culture score. The data presented a trend that the top nine schools, according to mean SAT-9 scores, had mean school culture scores near 1.5, which is a score representative of a strong school culture, according to the design of the School Culture Survey.

Results showed that math scores were higher on average than reading and language arts scores. The average math score for the study was in the 55th percentile rank. Scores for reading were in the 44th percentile rank for language arts. The data from the study suggested that math is a stronger subject for students in participating schools than the subjects of language arts and reading. This information may suggest that most students completing this particular test are secondary language learners. Data also might suggest that current reading and language arts curriculum and instruction methods are not as effective as current mathematics curriculum and instruction.

Research Question 3

Was there a relationship between school organizational culture as measured by the School Culture Survey and the results of standardized test scores in language arts, reading, and mathematics as measured by the SAT-9? A significant relationship was found between the perceived school organizational culture and student achievement. The results of this research showed that, based on the research questions, there was support for the stated hypothesis. The results showed a significant relationship between a school's organizational culture and the overall results of standardized test scores in language arts, reading, and mathematics as measured by the SAT-9. The results of the correlation concluded the populations were correlated with a correlation coefficient, $r = -.52$, $p < .05$. Overall results demonstrated that the correlation was significant; however, this was not necessarily true regarding subject-area correlations. Scores for language arts on the SAT-9 and mean culture scores correlated with a correlation coefficient, $r = -.67$, $p < .05$. However, results for math and reading did not follow a similar pattern. SAT-9 mean scores in mathematics correlated with mean culture scores indicated that the two populations were not correlated with the correlation coefficient, $r = -.28$, $p < .05$. The data regarding mean SAT-9 reading scores correlated with mean culture score results yielded similar findings, displayed in Figure 4. The results for the correlation between mean culture scores and SAT-9 mean reading scores showed that the populations were not correlated with a correlation coefficient, $r = -.48$, $p < .05$.

Although not every school was consistent with having a high culture score and high student achievement score, most schools were significant or consistent, with the culture score reflecting the relative results of the student achievement. Results of the research indicated that the higher the perception of culture, the greater the results of overall student achievement, with few exceptions to those results. These results support previous research findings that organizational culture is correlated with organizational effectiveness (Collins, 2004; Collins & Porras, 1997; Denison & Mishra, 1989; Heskett & Kotter, 1992). These results support previous research regarding the influence of school culture on increased student achievement (Goldring, 2002; Holmes, 2003; Marriot, 2001; Strahan, 2003). Empirical evidence suggests the culture of a business organization can influence productivity; hence, there is reason to believe similar cultural dimensions accounting for increased business performance may account for increased achievement in schools (Deal & Peterson, 1999a).

Conclusions

The purposes of this quantitative study were (a) to examine the perceived school culture for participating schools, (b) to review student achievement in participating school by examining the SAT-9 scores for participating schools, and (c) to determine if a relationship existed between the perceptions of school culture and student achievement in participating schools in southwest Arizona. Based on research findings and related literature, the following conclusions were drawn:

1. The mean scores on the school culture surveys completed by the teachers and administrators of participating schools indicated that the general perception of culture in all participating schools was relatively high. No culture score measured above a score of 2.33 on a scale of 1.0–4.0, with 1.0 indicating a positive culture score and 4.0 indicating a weak culture score.

2. Mean culture scores for participating schools did not indicate any significant influence from socioeconomic factors, school size, or population diversity. SAT-9 achievement test scores indicated no significant influence due to school size or population diversity. SAT-9 scores were lower in language arts and reading compared to overall scores in mathematics. This information may suggest that most students completing this particular test are secondary language learners. Data also suggested that current reading and language arts curriculum and instruction methods may not be as effective as current math curriculum and instruction.

3. Differences between cultural perceptions of teachers and administrators showed a significant difference regarding SAT-9 results. For instance, 80% of schools with a higher perception of culture, according to administrators, were in the top half of schools regarding SAT-9 scores, compared to 33% of schools with a higher perception of culture by teachers than by administrators.

4. Not every school reflected high culture scores and high student achievement scores, and vice versa. School 9 scored a high culture score but not high student achievement test scores, and School 15 scored a moderate culture score and relatively high student achievement scores. Examples are provided in Table 7.

5. The results showed a significant relationship between a school's organizational culture and the overall results of standardized test scores in language arts, reading, and mathematics as measured by the SAT-9. The results of the correlation concluded the populations were significantly correlated.

6. Participation of surveyed teachers had no relationship with mean culture scores. The mean culture scores showed a steady rise in scores from School 1 through

School 17. The percentage of teachers with 5 years of experience moves up and down throughout participating schools.

7.   Not every school reflected high culture scores and high student achievement scores, and vice versa. School 9 scored a high culture score but not high student achievement test scores, and School 15 scored a moderate culture score and relatively high student achievement scores. Examples are provided in Table 7. Schools 9 and 15 did not reflect typical results of the study, but such exceptions may lead to further research for school leaders. The results presented from the research questions and the conclusions may allow educators and constituents to use similar methods of research within their schools or school districts, which is explained further in the following section.

Table 7

Examples of Inconsistent School Culture Score and Stanford Achievement Test, Ninth Edition, Percentile Rank

School	Mean culture score	Mean Stanford Achievement Test score
School 15	2.19 (moderate)	55.1 (high)
School 9	1.77 (high)	33.0 (low)

Implications and Recommendations

School leadership is a field of constant change, and with the increased focus on higher curriculum standards and accountability, the current political and cultural climate demands that school leaders hold principals, teachers, and parents to the highest levels of accountability. The accountability in any school is the results of student achievement testing (Cunningham & Gresso, 1993). Although it is the current paradigm of achievement, standardized testing is essentially a snapshot of student ability, which may fail to recognize the essence of student potential, growth, or achievement in all academic subjects (Boyles, 2000; Olson, 2005; Wilson, 2005). Nevertheless, school administrators are required to focus on the results of testing as the measure of success.

Each school year begins with school leaders searching for the most exemplary and current educational practices to show significant student gains, and constructing and strengthening culture may be as important as material and philosophical educational resources. Basic management at the school district and building level implies that the tools and instruments of the trade hold the answers to student achievement improvement (Fullan, 1997). Leaders may desire to analyze the larger picture of school organizational health, including teacher training, hiring practices, and organizational culture, looking for the influence of those factors on academic student achievement. The shared beliefs of the constituency and the overall cultural manifestation of the school as an organization contribute to the perception of what the organization means to each member. Building a professional culture consistent with the aspects of any cultural research instrument and the data obtained from the instrument may allow change in the cultural perception of any school organization. The following are recommendations and implications for school district leaders, including school governing boards and superintendents, building-level principals, school curricular teams and subgroups, and the community at large.

Culture is described as the shared values, beliefs, and assumptions that shape an organization (Stolp & Smith, 1995). Understanding and recognizing the merit of culture will benefit any school district superintendent and elected governing board, because the entrenched culture will define and determine the opportunity for effective change and implementation of new programs, despite the hierarchy within the governance of the school district (Leithwood et al., 2001). The present study was developed to determine cultural perceptions of participating schools using a survey instrument designed to quantify cultural perceptions. Building shared vision within a new culture among the constituency of the school district, or perpetuating the current culture of the school district, is the mandate for any school administrator (Stolp & Smith). Shared vision allows the school district to plan all facets of business, including hiring staff, purchasing supplies, designing academic curricula, planning and scheduling for the school district, and developing long-term district goals.

The present research offered support for internal shared vision among participating schools, as mean culture scores on the School Culture Survey were relatively high. No culture score measured above a score of 2.33 on a scale of 1.0–4.0, with 1.0 indicating a positive, or strong cohesive culture score and 4.0 indicating a weak culture score. Considering this information, school leaders with the knowledge of cultural perception and the ability to obtain the data through surveys and interviews can include culture as a valuable resource for school improvement, as evidenced through similar research efforts (Akhavan, 2005; Craig et al., 2005; Reavis et al., 1999).

Knowledge of current cultural perceptions at the school building level can benefit principals because information can be used to develop and activate programs for change and improvement or sustain current successful practice. The opportunity to build and develop culture at the building level can be a difficult endeavor, because in many instances, teachers will remain at a school for several years, whereas principals are hired from an outside community or school and typically hold the position for 4–5 years (Senge

et al., 2000). Current teachers are perpetuating the current culture, and principals new to

the particular position must learn the culture and understand the nuances of the

community before changes commence. Building or rebuilding culture may have

casualties insofar as those unwilling to follow the new system may need dismissal or

reassignment.

The procedure and results of surveying teachers in this study may provide school

leaders with the knowledge necessary for accurate change in specific cultural ideas,

including professional collaboration and school discipline. Principals learning a culture

and attempting to change imbedded culture may confront this situation in the process.

Leadership in the principal position will confront difficult situations, and building culture

leading to measurable student success could translate to lasting school success. Shaping

school culture involves (a) developing a student-centered mission and purpose that

motivates the heads and hearts of staff, students, and community; (b) strengthening

elements of the existing culture that are positive and supportive of core values; (c)

building on the established traditions and values, by adding new, constructive ones to the

existing combination; (d) recruiting, hiring, and socializing staff who share the values of

the culture and who will add new insights or skills to the culture; (e) using the history of

the culture to fortify the core values and beliefs; and (f) sustaining core norms, values,

and beliefs in everything the school does (Deal & Peterson, 1999a).

In school districts, the building-level situation parallels the district-level situation,

but allows leadership to review and examine results on a smaller or more manageable

scale. Constructing a shared vision between district-level leadership and building-level leadership translates to an advantageous situation as ideas flow between entities more easily and progress tracking is more efficient (Senge et al., 2000).

School faculties commonly are divided into teams or departments. Within these departments, a unique and autonomous culture is developed. This is especially true when the department is very successful compared to other departments (Glasser, 1998). An example may be a large and active music program in a small school setting, or a math department that continually earns high scores on standardized testing compared to an English department that continually may earn low scores. Creating a shared vision within a school or school district often begins by breaking down the system and discovering the smaller units and current successes, which may spark further success. Encouraging successful departments within the school system to share and build a community, which encourages learning, leads to the development of culture and shared vision. In this present study, the findings on the relationship between culture and measurable achievement hold strong implications for school leaders. Mean SAT-9 scores correlated with overall mean culture scores, demonstrating that the relationship between culture and achievement is significant. Among participating schools, 75% scoring below a mean of 1.7, indicating a high culture score on the School Culture Survey, had a mean SAT-9 percentile rank score above the 50th percentile rank, with two schools scoring above the 60th percentile rank. Comparatively, 10 participating schools scored below the 50th percentile rank on overall mean SAT-9 scores; 8 of those schools scored above a mean 1.7, indicating a low culture score on the School Culture Survey.

Culture translates to the idea of shared vision, which has a significant influence on results (Heskett & Kotter 1992). Senge et al. (2000) explained that teachers ordinarily are taught to work as individuals, so staff development has to help them learn to work together as a team or comprehensive unit. The team-building and vision-sharing process is ongoing, and time works to build an esprit de corps, to learn new ways of teaching, and to unlearn old habits.

The community surrounding and supplying the school contributes to the school's culture. Schools, in turn, contribute to communities and largely reflect the dispositions, attitudes, and values of the community population. Essentially, schools reflect the history of, share virtues with, and give a sense of pride to the local populous (Deal & Peterson, 1999a).

School leaders may wish to look to parents as a source to contribute to the school culture and build a shared vision. A study of parent–school relationships by Smekar (1999) examined four attitudes: (a) Parents valued education because parents felt a strong belief that a good education guarantees the opportunity to work and make a living; (b) parents desired to help their children with school whether through homework or simply being aware of problems and events in the school; (c) parents wanted to assist in school and not by giving funds, but by giving time and assisting teachers with their work; and (d) parents wanted to feel comfortable at school activities and have less formal relationships with school staff so that problems can be discussed informally.

Parent relationships, and an appreciation for the overall community contribution to the sense of culture, allow school leaders to use outside resources to provide another outlet leading to school success. School leaders may wish to incorporate all constituents in a shared effort both to achieve results and to create an institution that produces widespread faith, hope, and shared vision. The knowledge required for shaping culture internally must be applied to linking the school to parents and other members of the community (Deal & Peterson, 1999a).

The pressure to perform well on standardized test scores confronts school leaders in this age of accountability. School leaders understanding the significance of culture, and culture's influence on organizational performance and outcomes may be able to plan and strategize methods and programs to enhance the professional culture of the organization. School leaders could review the data of this study, especially looking at data reflecting the perceptions of culture, synthesizing strategies to improve or maintain school programs. In the present study, the findings on the relationship between culture and measurable achievement hold strong implications for school leaders. Mean SAT-9 scores correlated with overall mean culture scores, suggesting a significant relationship between culture and achievement. This information may benefit future school leaders to emphasize culture as a contributor to measurable student achievement.

Recommendations for Future Research

This study could be replicated within the boundaries of a school district with multiple elementary or secondary schools to discover perceptions of culture within a solitary school district. The data produced by this kind of study could allow school leaders to analyze current perceptions of culture and develop ideas to change areas of concern.

Another research opportunity could be to replicate this study using another form of student achievement, including graduation rates, college entrance exam scores, or activity participation. Changing this particular variable in the study may aid leaders in analyzing other areas where deficiencies may lie. Although student achievement may be high in a school, activity participation may be low, and leaders may wish to discover and analyze reasons why this may occur.

Further ideas would be to replicate the study using a population of schools with similar student populations, including ethnicity, size, and economic level, and similar test score results. The current study used a variety of schools including standard kindergarten through Grades 4 or 5 elementary schools, rural kindergarten through Grade 8 schools, and common Grade 9–12 high schools. The only common thread between the schools in the study was geographic location. Using schools with a common thread may allow school leaders to view results in similar settings, which may be an important variable in the analysis of research data. Replicating the study between differing economic locations within the state of Arizona may provide interesting results and allow leaders to determine the influence of socioeconomic levels, language influence, or strong school district policies. Finally, the use of private or charter schools substituting for public schools may yield interesting results considering the differences between organizational methods and financial management.

Qualitative or mixed-method studies also may be considered. A qualitative study observing school culture over periods of leadership change and the influence of that change on student results may benefit teachers and subject departments. Observation of staff turnover through a defined period correlated with achievement test data may benefit colleges and universities in teacher preparation and leadership development within faculties. Qualitative analysis of leadership training in university principal and superintendent certificate programs may yield interesting results. Traditional certificate programs focus on school management techniques combined with leadership perspectives. The modern school leadership program may wish to consider business techniques, including examples of culture, as a means of training as to increase a principal or superintendent's knowledge base.

Summary

Chapter 5 provided explanations and conclusions of this research project. An overview of the problem statement was given, accompanied by a summary and discussion of findings, implications, and recommendations for school leaders, along with possibilities for future research. Research on organizational culture in the school setting and the correlation between perceptions of culture and student achievement results provide possibilities for research and an alternative path of leadership direction, perhaps leading toward greater measurable results for school leaders. Schools and school districts are under increasing pressure to perform under a business model, with student achievement test score results as the measure of quality. School leaders wishing to find a means of staff development with a comprehensive goal of faculty cohesiveness and a sense of oneness may consider culture and review the results of this study. Heskett and Kotter (1992) concluded from their evidence, "No matter how one looks at the issue, the economic and social consequences of unhealthy cultures looms large" (p. 92).

Leadership within in a school or any organization guides culture, and leaders are responsible for the results of that organization, despite the positive or negative influence culture provides. Politically and financially, test scores measure school success. The success of a child has become a quantitative formula rather than a qualitative observation, and school leaders acknowledging this paradigm and directing schools accordingly may find greater longevity in the profession.

REFERENCES

Akhavan, N. (2005). Creating and sustaining a collaborative culture: Lee Richmond School improved instruction by creating a culture where it is good to question instructional practices and commit to finding answers together. *Leadership, 34*(5), 3-20.

Altman, Y., & Baruch, Y. (1998). Cultural theory and organizations: Analytical method and cases. *Organization Studies, 19,* 769–785.

Alveeson, M. (1990). On the popularity of organizational culture. *Acta Sociologica, 33,* 31–49.

Arizona Department of Education. (n.d.). Home page. Available at http://www.ade.state .az.us

Arizona Department of Education. (2004). *State report: Arizona student achievement program.* Phoenix, AZ: Harcourt.

Badaracco, J., & Ellsworth, R. (2004). Leadership, integrity and conflict. *Journal of Organizational Change Management, 4,* 46–55.

Bagraim, J. (2001). Organizational psychology and workplace control: The instrumentality of corporate culture. *South African Journal of Psychology, 31,* 43.

Barret, R. (2003). Improve your cultural capital. *Industrial Management,* 20–24.

Bolman, L., & Deal, T. (1997). *Reframing organizations: Artistry, choice and leadership.* San Francisco: Jossey-Bass.

Boyles, D. (2000). *American education and corporations: The free market goes to school.* New York: Falmer Press.

Carnegie Council on Adolescent Development. (1989). *Turning points: Preparing American youth for the 21st century* New York: Carnegie Corporation.

Chen, L. Y. (2004). Examining the effect of organization culture and leadership behaviors on organizational commitment, job satisfaction, and job performance at small and middle-sized firms in Taiwan. *The Journal of American Academy of Business, Cambridge, 5,* 432–438.

Coleman, J. (2004). From at-risk to at-promise. *Principal, 84,* 30–34.

Collins, J. (2004). *Good to great.* New York: HarperCollins.

Collins, J., & Porras, J. (1997). *Built to last: Successful habits of visionary companies.* New York: Harper Business.

Craig, J., Butler, A., Cairo, L., III, Wood, C., Gilchrist, C., Holloway, J., et al. (2005). *A case study of six high-performing schools in Tennessee.* Charleston, WV: Appalachia Educational Laboratory.

Creswell, J. (2003). *Research design: Qualitative, quantitative, and mixed method approaches* (2nd ed.). Thousand Oaks, CA: Sage.

Cunningham, W., & Gresso, D. (1993) *Cultural leadership: The culture of excellence in education.* Needham Heights, MA: Allyn and Bacon.

Deal, T., & Kennedy, A. (1982). *Corporate culture: The rites and rituals of corporate life.* Boston: Addison-Wesley.

Deal, T., & Peterson, K. (1999a). *Shaping school culture: The heart of leadership.* San Francisco: Jossey-Bass.

Deal, T., & Peterson, K. (1999b). *Shaping school culture.* San Francisco: Jossey-Bass.

Denison, D., & Mishra, A. (1989). Organizational culture and organizational effectiveness: A theory and some preliminary empirical evidence. *Organization Science, 6*(2), 204-223.

Detert, J. (2000). A framework for linking culture and improvement initiatives in organizations. *Academy of Management Review, 25,* 850.

Duques, R., & Gaske, P. (1997). The "big" organization of the future. In F. Hesselbein, M. Goldsmith, & R. Beckhard (Eds.), *The organization of the future* (pp. 33–42). San Francisco: Jossey-Bass.

Finnerman, K. (2003). Testy about testing. *Issues in Science and Technology, 19.*

Fritzberg, G. (2004). Revise and resubmit: A critical response to Title 1 of the No Child Left Behind Act. *Journal of Education, 184.*

Fullan, M. (1997). *What's worth fighting for in the principalship.* New York: Teachers College Press.

Gall, M. D., Borg, W. R., & Gall, J. P. (1996). *Educational research: An introduction.* White Plains, NY: Longman.

Geertz, C. (1973). *Interpretation of cultures.* New York: Basic Books.

Glasser, W. (1998). *The quality school teacher* (rev. ed.) San Francisco: HarperCollins.

Glickman, C. (2003). Symbols and celebrations that sustain education. *Educational Leadership, 60,* 34–38.

Goldring, L. (2002). The power of school culture. *Leadership, 32,* 32–35.

Hall, G., & Hord, S. (2001). *Implementing change: Patterns, principles, and potholes.* Needham Heights, MA: Allyn and Bacon.

Hanson, D., & Lackman, C. (2001). Managing through cultural differences. *CR, 8,* 46–53.

Harcourt Assessment, Inc. (2004). *Technical information on test scores.* San Antonio, TX: PsychCorp.

Hatch, M. J. (1997). *Organization theory: Modern symbolic and postmodern perspectives.* New York: Oxford University Press.

Heskett, J., & Kotter, J. (1992). *Corporate culture and performance.* New York: Free Press.

Hofstede, G., Neuijen, D., Ohayv, D., & Sanders, G. (1990). Measuring organizational cultures: A qualitative and quantitative study across twenty cases. *Administrative Science Quarterly, 35,* 286–316.

Holmes, N. (2000). *Learning to lead, leading to learn.* Retrieved June 30, 2004, from the American Association of School Administrators Web site: http://www.aasa.org

Holmes, N. (2003). *Leadership teams help district focus, progress toward higher achievement.* Retrieved June 30, 2004, from the American Association of School Administrators Web site: http://www.aasa.org

Jackson, S. (2003). Commentary on the rhetoric of reform: A twenty year prospective. In K. Saltman & D. Gabbard (Eds.), *Education as reinforcement: The militarization and corporatization of schools.* New York: Routledge Falmer.

Kotter, J., Sasser E., & Schlesinger, L. (1997). *The service profit chain: How leading companies link profit and growth to loyalty, satisfaction, and value.* New York: The Free Press.

Kucerik, E. (2002). The No Child Left Behind Act of 2001: Will it live up to its promise? *Georgetown Journal on Poverty Law and Policy, 9,* 479–487.

Lashway, L. (2001). *Developing instructional leaders.* Retrieved June 30, 2004, from the University Library Web site: http://www.apollolibrary.com

Leatherman, J. (2004, August). Students' reading skills improve: Yuma County school assessing test scores. *The Sun.*

Leedy, P. D., & Ormond, J. E. (2001). *Practical research: Planning and design* (7th ed.). Upper Saddle River, NJ: Merrill Prentice Hall.

Leithwood, K., Aitken, R., & Jantzi, D. (2001). *Making schools smarter: A system for monitoring school and district progress* (2nd ed.). Thousand Oaks, CA: Sage.

Lucas, S., Quinn, D., Miles, M., Valentine, J., & Gawerecki, J. (2002). *Four components for meaningful, continuous school improvement.* Arlington, VA: National Association of Secondary School Principals.

Marriot, D. (2001). Managing school culture. *Principal-Urban and Rural: The Challenged Schools, 81,* 1–3.

Marshall, C., & Rossman, G. (1999). *Designing qualitative research* (3rd ed.). Thousand Oaks, CA: Sage.

McNeil, L. (2000a). *Contradictions of school reform: Educational costs of standardized testing.* New York: Routledge.

McNeil, L. (2000b). Creating new inequalities: Contradictions of reform. *Phi Delta Kappan, 81,* 729–734.

Melendez, M., & Konig, R. (2004, August 17). Stanford 9 scores improve: Arizona's 9th-graders still struggling with reading. *The Arizona Republic.*

Miller, K. L. (2004). Best of the best. *Newsweek, 143,* 42–47.

Morgan, G. (1998). *Images of organization: The executive edition.* London: Sage.

Murphy, J., & Louis, K. S. (1999). *Handbook of research on educational administration*
(2nd ed.). San Francisco: Jossey-Bass.

Nelson, J., Carlson, K., & Palonsky, S. (1996). *Critical issues in education: A dialectic
approach* (3rd ed.). New York: McGraw-Hill.

Ogbonna, E. (2001). The founder's legacy: Hangover or inheritance. *British Journal of
Management, 12,* 13–19.

Olson, A. (2005). Improving schools one student at a time. *Educational Leadership,
62*(5), 37-40.

Perkinson, H. J. (1995). *The imperfect panacea: American faith in education* (4th ed.).
Boston: McGraw-Hill.

Peters, T. J., & Waterman, R. H. (1982). *In search of excellence.* New York: Harper &
Row.

Peterson, K. (2002). Positive or negative? *Journal of Staff Development 23(3).*

Pondy, L., & Mitroff, I. (1979). Research in organizational behavior. *Research in
Organizational Behavior, 1,* 3–39.

Protheroe, N., & Perkins-Gough, D. (2001). *Essentials for principals: Meeting the
challenges of high-stakes testing.* Alexandria, VA: National Association of
Elementary School Principals.

Queen, J. A. (1999). *Curriculum practice in the elementary and middle school.*
Columbus, OH: Merrill.

Reavis, C. A., Vinson, D., & Fox, R. (1999). Importing a culture of success via a strong

    principal. *The Clearing House, 72*(4), 199-202.

Rollins, T., & Roberts, D. (1998). *Work culture, organizational performance, and*

    business success: Measurement and management. London: Quorum Books.

Sacks, P. (1999). *Standardized minds.* New York: Perseus Books.

Saphier, J., & King, M. (1985). Good seeds grow in strong cultures. *Educational*

    Leadership, 42, 67–74.

Saranson, S. (1982). *The culture of the school and the problem of change.* Boston: Allyn

    & Bacon.

Schein, E. H. (1992). *Organizational culture and leadership* (2nd ed.). San Francisco:

    Jossey-Bass.

Scherer, M. (2001). Improving the quality of the teaching force: A conversation with

    David C. Berliner. *Education Leadership, 58,* 6-10.

Schmoker, M. (2000). *Results: The key to continuous school improvement* (2nd ed.).

    Alexandria, VA: ASCD.

Senge, P., Chambron-McCabe, N., Lucas, T., Smith, B., Dutton, J., & Kleiner, A. (2000).

    Schools that learn: A fifth discipline fieldbook for educators, parents, and

    everyone who cares about education. New York: Currency-Doubleday.

Sergiovanni, T. J. (2000). *The lifeworld of leadership creating culture, community, and*

    personal meaning in our schools. San Francisco: Jossey-Bass.

Shann, M. (1999). Academics and a culture of caring: The relationship between school

    achievement and prosocial and antisocial behaviors in four urban middle schools.

    School Effectiveness and School Improvement, 10, 390–413.

Smekar, C. (1996). *The impact of school choice and community: In the interest of families and schools.* New York: University of New York Press

Smircich, L. (1985). Is the concept of culture a paradigm for understanding organizations and ourselves? In P. J. Frost, L. F. Moore, M. R. Louis, C. C. Lundberg, & J. Martin (Eds.), *Organizational culture* (pp. 35–72). Beverly Hills, CA: Sage.

Smith, C. (2000). Organizational culture in practice. *Human Resource Development International, 3,* 153–158.

Smith, M. L., & Glass, G. (1987). *Research and evaluation in education and the social sciences.* Needham Heights, MA: Allyn and Bacon.

Stolp, S. (1994). Leadership for school culture. *ERIC digest.* Retrieved June 30, 2004, http:// www.eric.ed.gov.

Stolp, S., & Smith, S. C. (1995). *Transforming school culture: Stories, symbols, values and the leader's role.* Eugene: University of Oregon.

Strahan, D. (2003). Promoting a collaborative culture in three elementary schools that have beaten the odds. *The Elementary School Journal, 104,* 127.

Taylor, R. (2002). Shaping the culture of learning communities. *Principal Leadership, 3,* 42.

Tobergte, D. R., & Curtis, S. (2002). There is a crisis! and failure is not an option. *Education, 122,* 770.

Trice, H., & Beyer, J. (1993). *The cultures of work organizations.* Upper Saddle River, NJ: Prentice Hall.

Triola, M. (2001). *Elementary statistics* (8th ed.). Boston: Addison Wesley Longman.

U.S. Department of Education. (2002). *The No Child Left Behind Act of 2001: Executive summary*. Washington, DC: Author.

University of Phoenix. (2002). *Research handbook* [pamphlet]. Phoenix, AZ: Apollo Group.

Valle, M. (1999). Crisis, culture, and charisma: The new leader's work in public organizations. *Public Personnel Management, 28,* 245–257.

Vogt, W. P. (1999). *Dictionary of statistics and methodology: A nontechnical guide to the social sciences* (2nd ed.). Thousand Oaks, CA: Sage.

Wilson, R. (2005), Targeted growth for every student. *Leadership*, (35)2, p8.

APPENDIX A: RESEARCH REVIEW

Key term search	Research tool	Researched locations	No. of related references (no. used)
Culture	Reference Manager (RM) 11	430 databases	81 (47)
Organizational culture	RM 11	430 databases	3 (0)
Corporate culture	RM 11	430 databases	10 (5)
School	RM 11	430 database	21 (8)
School culture	RM 11	430 databases	15 (2)
Standardized testing	RM 11	430 databases	25 (5)
School leadership	RM 11	430 databases	15 (2)
Curriculum	RM 11	430 databases	3 (0)
Leadership	RM 11	430 databases	37 (3)
Critical theory	RM 11	430 databases	5 (3)
Synthesis of search	RM 11		265 (75)
Organizational culture	ERIC	ERIC database	369 (3)
School culture	ERIC	ERIC database	20 (3)
Standardized testing success	ERIC	ERIC database	5 (0)
School leadership and culture	ERIC	ERIC database	7 (2)
Synthesis of search	ERIC		401 (5)

Searches through the ERIC database are full-text only. Although a large number of articles are displayed, many are not available full text.

APPENDIX B: SIGNED INFORMED CONSENT

Permission to use survey from Wellton Elementary School, Wellton Elementary School

District #24.

UNIVERSITY OF PHOENIX

INFORMED CONSENT: PERMISSION TO USE PREMISES

(Facility, Organization, University, Institution, or Association)

Hyder Elementary School District
Wellton Elementary School District
Antelope Union High School District
Mohawk Valley Elementary School District
Yuma Elementary School District
Yuma Union High School District
Somerton Elementary School District
Gadsden Elementary School District
Crane Elementary School District

Name of Facility, Organization, University, Institution, or Association

I hereby authorize Andrew L. Smith, student of University of Phoenix, to use the facilities requested to conduct a study entitled A Study of the relationship between school culture and standardized test scores.

_____   7-6-04
Signature   ▬▬▬▬
                                        Date

Title _Superintendent_

This permission allows the researcher to survey all school sites within the school district marked with an X above.
Name of Facility

113

Permission to use survey from Somerton Elementary School District. The district is

comprised of four schools used for the study: (a) Somerton Middle School, (b) Desert

Sonora Elementary School, (c) Tierra Del Sol Elementary School, and (d) Orange Grove

Elementary School.

UNIVERSITY OF PHOENIX

INFORMED CONSENT: PERMISSION TO USE PREMISES
(Facility, Organization, University, Institution, or Association)

Hyder Elementary School District
Wellton Elementary School District
Antelope Union High School District
Mohawk Valley Elementary School District
Yuma Elementary School District
Yuma Union High School District
Somerton Elementary School District X
Gadsden Elementary School District
Crane Elementary School District

Name of Facility, Organization, University, Institution, or Association

I hereby authorize Andrew L. Smith, student of University of Phoenix, to use the facilities requested to conduct a study entitled A Study of the relationship between school culture and standardized test scores.

Signature _____   Date _____ 2004

Title   Superintendent

This permission allows the researcher to survey all school sites within the school district marked with an X above.
Name of Facility

114

Permission to use survey from Yuma Union High School District comprising of three

high schools: (a) Yuma High School, (b) Cibola High School, and (c) Kofa High School.

UNIVERSITY OF PHOENIX

INFORMED CONSENT: PERMISSION TO USE PREMISES

(Facility, Organization, University, Institution, or Association)

Hyder Elementary School District _____
Wellton Elementary School District _____
Antelope Union High School District _____
Mohawk Valley Elementary School District _____
Yuma Elementary School District _____
Yuma Union High School District   X _____
Somerton Elementary School District _____
Gadsden Elementary School District _____
Crane Elementary School District _____
Palo Verde Elementary School District _____
Sentinel Elementary School District _____

Name of Facility, Organization, University, Institution, or Association

I hereby authorize Andrew L. Smith, student of University of Phoenix, to use the facilities requested to conduct a study entitled A Study of the relationship between school culture and standardized test scores.

_____   7-23-04   ▮▮▮▮▮
Signature   Date

Assistant Superintendent, Yuma Union High School District
Title

This permission allows the researcher to survey all school sites within the school district marked with an X above.
Name of Facility

115

Permission to use survey from Sentinel Elementary School, Sentinel Elementary School

District.

UNIVERSITY OF PHOENIX

INFORMED CONSENT: PERMISSION TO USE PREMISES

(Facility, Organization, University, Institution, or Association)

Hyder Elementary School District
Wellton Elementary School District
Antelope Union High School District
Mohawk Valley Elementary School District
Yuma Elementary School District
Yuma Union High School District
Somerton Elementary School District
Gadsden Elementary School District
Crane Elementary School District
Palo Verde Elementary School District
X Sentinel Elementary School District

Name of Facility, Organization, University, Institution, or Association

I hereby authorize Andrew L. Smith, student of University of Phoenix, to use the facilities requested to conduct a study entitled A Study of the relationship between school culture and standardized test scores.

Signature

Date

Title   DISTRICT ADMINISTRATOR

This permission allows the researcher to survey all school sites within the school district marked with an X above.

Name of Facility

116

Permission to use survey from Mohawk Valley Elementary School, Mohawk Valley

Elementary School District.

UNIVERSITY OF PHOENIX

INFORMED CONSENT: PERMISSION TO USE PREMISES

(Facility, Organization, University, Institution, or Association)

Hyder Elementary School District
Wellton Elementary School District
Antelope Union High School District
Mohawk Valley Elementary School District   X
Yuma Elementary School District
Yuma Union High School District
Somerton Elementary School District
Gadsden Elementary School District
Crane Elementary School District

Name of Facility, Organization, University, Institution, or Association

I hereby authorize Andrew L. Smith, student of University of Phoenix, to use the facilities requested to conduct a study entitled A Study of the relationship between school culture and standardized test scores.

Signature   7-12-04
                                            Date

Title   Superintendent

This permission allows the researcher to survey all school sites within the school district marked with an X above.
Name of Facility

117

Permission to use survey from Dateland Elementary School, Hyder Elementary School District.

UNIVERSITY OF PHOENIX

INFORMED CONSENT: PERMISSION TO USE PREMISES

(Facility, Organization, University, Institution, or Association)

Hyder Elementary School District   X
Walton Elementary School District
Antelope Union High School District
Mohawk Valley Elementary School District
Yuma Elementary School District
Yuma Union High School District
Somerton Elementary School District
Gadsden Elementary School District
Crane Elementary School District

Name of Facility, Organization, University, Institution, or Association

I hereby authorize Andrew L. Smith, student of University of Phoenix, to use the facilities requested to conduct a study entitled A Study of the relationship between school culture and standardized test scores.

Signature

Date   7/7/04

Title   Superintendent

This permission allows the researcher to survey all school sites within the school district marked with an X above.
Name of Facility

118

Permission to use survey from Antelope Union High School, Antelope Union High School District.

UNIVERSITY OF PHOENIX

INFORMED CONSENT: PERMISSION TO USE PREMISES

(Facility, Organization, University, Institution, or Association)

Hyder Elementary School District
Wellton Elementary School District
Antelope Union High School District   RK
Mohawk Valley Elementary School District
Yuma Elementary School District
Yuma Union High School District
Somerton Elementary School District
Gadsden Elementary School District
Crane Elementary School District

Name of Facility, Organization, University, Institution, or Association

I hereby authorize <u>Andrew L. Smith</u>, student of University of Phoenix, to use the facilities requested to conduct a study entitled A Study of the relationship between school culture and standardized test scores.

Robert Klee   8/7/04

Signature   Date

Title Superintendent

This permission allows the researcher to survey all school sites within the school district marked with an X above.

Name of Facility

119

Permission to approach principals within the Yuma Elementary School District #1.

UNIVERSITY OF PHOENIX

INFORMED CONSENT: PERMISSION TO USE PREMISES

(Facility, Organization, University, Institution, or Association)

Hyder Elementary School District
Wellton Elementary School District
Antelope Union High School District
Mohawk Valley Elementary School District
Yuma Elementary School District
Yuma Union High School District
Somerton Elementary School District
Gadsden Elementary School District
Crane Elementary School District

Name of Facility, Organization, University, Institution, or Association

I hereby authorize Andrew L. Smith, student of University of Phoenix, to use the facilities requested to conduct a study entitled A Study of the relationship between school culture and standardized test scores. *You must have permission from the principal at each school.*

Vivian M. Eglert
Signature

Date

August 2, 2004

Title *Superintendent, Yuma Elem. Sch. District #1*

This permission allows the researcher to survey all school sites within the school district marked with an X above.
Name of Facility

Permission to use survey from Alice Byrne Elementary School, Yuma Elementary School

District #1.

Permission to use survey from Desert Mesa Elementary School, Yuma Elementary

School District #1.

UNIVERSITY OF PHOENIX

INFORMED CONSENT: PERMISSION TO USE PREMISES

(Facility, Organization, University, Institution, or Association)

Hyder Elementary School District
Wellton Elementary School District
Antelope Union High School District
Mohawk Valley Elementary School District
Yuma Elementary School District   X
Yuma Union High School District
Somerton Elementary School District
Gadsden Elementary School District
Crane Elementary School District
Palo Verde Elementary School District
Sentinal Elementary School District

Name of Facility, Organization, University, Institution, or Association

I hereby authorize Andrew L. Smith, student of University of Phoenix, to use the facilities requested to conduct a study entitled A Study of the relationship between school culture and standardized test scores.

Signature _____   Date 8/5/04

Title Principal: Desert Mesa   School Name _____

This permission allows the researcher to survey all school sites within the school district marked with an X above.
Name of Facility

122

Permission to use survey from Palmcroft Elementary School, Yuma Elementary School

District #1.

Signature _____   Date 8/13/04

Title _____   _Palmcroft_
School Name

This permission allows the researcher to survey all school sites within the school district marked with an X above.
Name of Facility

123

Email correspondence from Cindy Didway, superintendent of Crane Elementary School

District.

Feel free to contact the principals individually and ask for their participation. I will leave it up to them to participate if they want to.
Cindy
----- Original Message -----
From: "ANDREW SMITH" <smithboy@email.uophx.edu>
To: <cdidway@crane.apscc.k12.az.us>
Cc: "ANDREW SMITH" <smithboy@email.uophx.edu>
Sent: Friday, July 30, 2004 1:47 PM
Subject: Wellton principal dissertation study

> Mrs. Didway
> My name is Andy Smith and I am the principal at Wellton Elementary.
> Recently, I dropped off an information packet to you regarding my
> dissertation study that I am completing as part of my Doctor of Management
> degree at University of Phoenix. The study is a survey of school culture in
> Yuma County schools and a comparison of those results to Stanford 9 scores
> from the 2003-2004 school year.
>
> I am asking permission to survey the schools in the Crane district to
> measure school culture. The survey is very simple and only 38 questions. I
> would like to survey the principal and teachers in each school. Schools
> under 3 years will not be used. The total time to complete the survey
> should not be more than 10 minutes, and a minimum of 5 participants in each
> school would suffice.
>
> The final dissertation will not use any school names and each participant
> will be anonymous.
>
> I hope will you consider allowing me to complete my study.
>
> The information packet has a permission form if you allow me to use the
> Crane district, and if you allow me
> I am asking you to return that form to me via fax at: [fax number] and if you
> have not reviewed the packet I can bring another to you at your district
> office or email you the information packet. I am also available to meet
> with you, or phone conference at [phone number].
>
> If you are not interested will you please return this email indicating so.
> Thank you so much for your time.
> Andy

Permission to use survey at Centennial Middle School, Crane Elementary School District.

UNIVERSITY OF PHOENIX

INFORMED CONSENT: PERMISSION TO USE PREMISES

(Facility, Organization, University, Institution, or Association)

Hyder Elementary School District
Wellton Elementary School District
Antelope Union High School District
Mohawk Valley Elementary School District
Yuma Elementary School District
Yuma Union High School District
Somerton Elementary School District
Gadsden Elementary School District
Crane Elementary School District ___X___
Palo Verde Elementary School District
Sentinel Elementary School District

Name of Facility, Organization, University, Institution, or Association

I hereby authorize Andrew L. Smith, student of University of Phoenix, to use the facilities requested to conduct a study entitled A Study of the relationship between school culture and standardized test scores.

_____   _____
Signature   Date

_____   _____
Title   School name

This permission allows the researcher to survey all school sites within the school district marked with an X above.
Name of Facility

1

125

UNIVERSITY OF PHOENIX

INFORMED CONSENT: PERMISSION TO USE PREMISES

(Facility, Organization, University, Institution, or Association)

Hyder Elementary School District
Wellton Elementary School District
Antelope Union High School District
Mohawk Valley Elementary School District
Yuma Elementary School District
Yuma Union High School District
Somerton Elementary School District
Gadsden Elementary School District
Crane Elementary School District
Palo Verde Elementary School District   X
Sentinel Elementary School District

Name of Facility, Organization, University, Institution, or Association

I hereby authorize Andrew L. Smith, student of University of Phoenix, to use the facilities requested to conduct a study entitled A Study of the relationship between school culture and standardized test scores.

Robert Aldridge 7/12/04   Principal

Signature   Date

Title

This permission allows the researcher to survey all school sites within the school district marked with an X above.
Name of Facility

UNIVERSITY OF PHOENIX

INFORMED CONSENT: PARTICIPANTS 18 YEARS OF AGE AND OLDER

This sample cover letter may be used as a general guide to fulfill the requirements of informed consent. Items in bold typeface or underlined must be written specific to the research study.

Dear Prospective Teacher/Administrator Interviewee,

I am a student at the University of Phoenix working on a Doctor of Management degree. I am conducting a research study entitled *A STUDY OF THE RELATIONSHIP BETWEEN SCHOOL ORGANIZATIONAL CULTURE AND STANDARDIZED TEST SCORES*. The purpose of the research study is to identify the organizational practices, professional rapport, and cultural artifacts, which lead to the identification of school organizational culture. The study will correlate the findings of school culture and standardized test scores, grouping by school size and clusters (elementary-middle-high schools) and culture perceptions between teachers and administrators for participating institutions.

Your participation will involve completing the School Culture Survey by Kenneth Leithwood, the assisting demographic information, and returning the completed form to the researcher. Anonymity of participant and school will be respected at all times, as each school will be designated either a letter or a number in the conclusion of the research. Your participation in this study is voluntary. If you choose not to participate or to withdraw from the study at any time, you can do so without penalty or loss of benefit to yourself. The results of the research study may be published but your name will not be used and your results will be maintained in confidence.

Although there may be no direct benefit to you, the possible benefit of your participation is invaluable providing educational leaders an opportunity to view the relationship between school organizational culture and respective school data aforementioned.

If you have any questions concerning the research study, please call me at [phone number].

Sincerely,

_____

Andrew L. Smith, Researcher

UNIVERSITY OF PHOENIX

PERMISSION TO USE AN EXISTING SURVEY

Date: 8/06/03

Mr.   Andrew L. Smith
Address: PO Box 262
               Wellton, AZ 85356

Thank you for your request for permission to use School Culture Survey (please review the correspondence from the publisher in Appendix C-b.) in your research study. We are willing to allow you to reproduce the instrument as outlined in your letter with the following understanding:

- You will use this survey only for your research study and will not sell or use it with any compensated management/curriculum development activities.

- You will include the copyright statement on all copies of the instrument.

- You will send your research study and one copy of reports, articles, and the like that make use of this survey data promptly to our attention.

If these are acceptable terms and conditions, please indicate so by signing one copy of this letter and returning it to us.

Best wishes with your study.

Sincerely,

_____
Signature

I understand these conditions and agree to abide by these terms and conditions.

Signed_____Date 8/06/03

Expected date of completion 10/30/04

SAGE PUBLICATIONS, INC.
CORWIN PRESS, INC.
PINE FORGE PRESS

REPRINT PERMISSION AGREEMENT/INVOICE

2455 TELLER RD., THOUSAND OAKS, CA 91320
OFFICE: (805) 499 –0721 EXT. 7716 FAX: (805) 375 1718
E-MAIL: PERMISSIONS@SAGEPUB.COM
FEDERAL TAX ID#95-2454902

Effective Date: August 1, 2003

SAGE REFERENCE #: SRN 080103 0033/85203/CORWIN
(This number must appear on all correspondence and payment of fees.)
EMAIL: PHONE #: 928-785-3311 FAX #: 928-785-3546
RE :

Smith, Andrew L.
Wellton Elementary School
PO Box 517
Wellton, Arizona 85356
United States

One-time only, non-exclusive, world rights in English are hereby granted to Smith, Andrew L. (hereafter referred to as "The Requester") for the following selection:

BOOK/JOURNAL TITLE:	MAKING SCHOOLS SMARTER (2ND ED); A SYSTEM FORMONITORING SCHOOL AND DISTRICT PROGRESS
AUTHOR/EDITOR:	LEITHWOOD
VOLUME/ISSUE #	
USE OF MATERIAL:	Dissertation
TITLE OF SELECTION:	SCHOOL CULTURE SURVEY
TYPE OF EXCERPT:	scale **EXCERPT:** PP 136-137
MAXIMUM PRINT RUN:	300
AMOUNT DUE:	*PER COPY: $0/scale
	*FLAT FEE: $0 *(If Per Copy & Flat Fee=$0, NO FEE.)

Permission is hereby granted under the following terms and conditions:

1. The number of copies must not exceed the copies as stated in the request, nor the Maximum Print Run stated on this agreement. If the Maximum Print Run is "unspecified," the number of copies hereby defaults to under 100 copies for institutional use, and 3,500 copies for commercial use. If requester requests 100 or more copies and the actual copies made drops below 100, the charge is $1 per copy
2. Permission is granted for prospective non-electronic print format only to be used after the date above. Use of selections in electronic media such as, but not limited to the Internet, Intranet, or CD-ROM is prohibited. However, permission is granted for transcription via non-standard size audio tape for use with the blind or visually impaired.
3. If the selection is to be reprinted for commercial use, one (1) copy must be submitted to Sage Publications, Inc. and one (1) copy provided to the author of the material, upon publication of the work. Use of selections in "course packs" for use in an educational setting are exempt from this clause.
4. The permission does not apply to any interior material not controlled by Sage Publications, Inc.
5. *Unless otherwise noted in your request,* the Flat Fee is based on a maximum print run of 3,500 copies. If the print run exceeds 3,500 copies, this agreement is automatically rescinded, and the request must be re-submitted, stating the correct print run.
6. If the selection is intended for use in a Master's Thesis and Doctoral Dissertation, additional permission is granted for the selection to be included in the printing of said scholarly work as part of UMI's "Books on Demand" program.
7. Full acknowledgment of your source must appear in every copy of your work as follows:
   Author(s), Book/Journal Title (Journal Volume Number and Issue Number)
   pp. xx-xx, copyright (c) 19xx by (Copyright Holder)
   Reprinted by Permission of (Publisher - either Sage Publications or Corwin Press), Inc.
8. Unless specified in the request or by prior arrangement with Sage Publications, Inc., payment is due from the Requester within sixty (60) days of the effective date of the agreement or upon publication of the book/journal, otherwise the agreement will automatically be rescinded without further notice.
9. Payment is to be made by Check or Money Order only, with the complete Sage Reference Number listed on the check or check stub. **We do not accept Purchase Orders or Credit Cards, nor do we create separate invoices.**
10. It is assumed that the requester is using the selection in question, and is subject to billing and collections procedures, unless otherwise noted in the signature on the right hand side of this agreement, or the requester informs Sage Publications, Inc. in writing.
11. ADDITIONAL PROVISIONS:

Your signature below constitutes full acceptance
of the terms and conditions of the agreement herein.

Andrew L. Smith
Signature of Requester
8.06.03
Date

Your signature below constitutes your rejection
of the terms and conditions of the agreement herein.

Signature of Requester

Date:

PLEASE REMIT ONE (1) SIGNED COPY OF THE AGREEMENT,
ALONG WITH ANY APPLICABLE PAYMENT TO THE ADDRESS LISTED ABOVE. THANK YOU.

APPENDIX D: COPY OF SURVEY INSTRUMENT

School Culture

Respondent Role:

☐ STUDENT
☐ TEACHER
☐ ADMINISTRATOR
☐ SUPPORT STAFF (Secretary, Custodian, School Assistant, etc.)
☐ PARENT
☐ TRUSTEE
☐ COMMUNITY MEMBER (other than parent)
☐ OTHER (specify)

INSTRUCTIONS TO RESPONDENTS:

The purpose of this survey is to obtain information about what you think of certain aspects of the school giving the survey. The information will be used in an effort to improve education for students. Therefore, please read the instructions carefully and answer each question as honestly as possible. You should be able to complete this survey in about 5 minutes. Your response to the questionnaire will be anonymous and will be combined with those of others to reveal patterns. Responses from your school will be combined with responses from other schools.

We are interested in the extent to which you agree or disagree with the following statements.
For each statement, select and check ONE of the following responses:

1	2	3	4	NA
strongly agree	agree	disagree	strongly disagree	not applicable/ don't know

	strongly agree			strongly disagree	
	1	2	3	4	NA
2.1 Strength					
1. Most teachers in our school share a similar set of values, beliefs, and attitudes related to teaching and learning.	☐	☐	☐	☐	☐
2. I have close working relationships with my colleagues in our school.	☐	☐	☐	☐	☐
3. There is ongoing, collaborative work among teachers in our school/department.	☐	☐	☐	☐	☐
4. Our school administrators share teachers' values, beliefs, and attitudes related to teaching and learning.	☐	☐	☐	☐	☐
5. There is a strong, positive relationship between students and staff in our school.	☐	☐	☐	☐	☐
6. Our school celebrates the achievements of staff and students.	☐	☐	☐	☐	☐
2.2 Form					
7. I have frequent conversations about teaching practices with colleagues in our school.	☐	☐	☐	☐	☐
8. I frequently work with colleague(s) in our school to prepare unit outlines and/or instructional materials.	☐	☐	☐	☐	☐
9. I share my professional expertise by demonstrating new teaching practices for colleagues.	☐	☐	☐	☐	☐
10. We observe each other teaching and then discuss our observations to gain better understanding of our own teaching strategies.	☐	☐	☐	☐	☐
11. I adhere to school curriculum decisions agreed on in collaboration with my colleagues.	☐	☐	☐	☐	☐

Copy of original

School Culture Survey page 1.

2.3.1 Content is safe and orderly

12. I usually work through problems with my students, rather than refer them to the administration.   ☐ ☐ ☐ ☐ ☐
13. I feel safe in our school.   ☐ ☐ ☐ ☐ ☐
14. Students feel safe in our school.   ☐ ☐ ☐ ☐ ☐
15. Our school is virtually free of vandalism.   ☐ ☐ ☐ ☐ ☐
16. Our school monitors student behavior.   ☐ ☐ ☐ ☐ ☐
17. I feel comfortable interacting with the students in our school.   ☐ ☐ ☐ ☐ ☐
18. Our school has relatively few discipline problems.   ☐ ☐ ☐ ☐ ☐
19. Inappropriate student behavior is dealt with effectively in our school.
20. The consequences for inappropriate behavior in our school are immediate and consistent.   ☐ ☐ ☐ ☐ ☐

2.3.2 Content is positive

21. Our school emphasizes creating a positive atmosphere for our students.   ☐ ☐ ☐ ☐ ☐
22. Our staff praise and reward students' exemplary efforts and behavior.   ☐ ☐ ☐ ☐ ☐

2.3.3 Content is student centered

23. Students in our school need to meet or exceed clearly defined expectations.   ☐ ☐ ☐ ☐ ☐
24. I meet with students informally outside school hours.   ☐ ☐ ☐ ☐ ☐
25. I hold high expectations for individual student learning and behavior.   ☐ ☐ ☐ ☐ ☐
26. I model lifelong learning for my students.   ☐ ☐ ☐ ☐ ☐
27. Our school recognizes teachers who are exemplary in their classroom and schoolwide practices.   ☐ ☐ ☐ ☐ ☐
28. Our school administration acts in the best interests of the individual students.   ☐ ☐ ☐ ☐ ☐

2.3.4 Content fosters learning for students

29. Planning for and helping students learn is my most important work.   ☐ ☐ ☐ ☐ ☐
30. My school administrators protect my classroom instructional time.   ☐ ☐ ☐ ☐ ☐
31. My colleagues make effective use of classroom time.   ☐ ☐ ☐ ☐ ☐

2.3.5 Content is designed to provide a professional work environment for staff

32. Strong, positive relationships between staff and school administration facilitate implementation of new programs.   ☐ ☐ ☐ ☐ ☐
33. I frequently implement new programs or new teaching strategies.   ☐ ☐ ☐ ☐ ☐
34. I engage in ongoing, professional development for myself.   ☐ ☐ ☐ ☐ ☐
35. I am motivated to implement new programs.   ☐ ☐ ☐ ☐ ☐
36. I am satisfied with my job.   ☐ ☐ ☐ ☐ ☐
37. Administrators in my school encourage professional risk taking and experimentation.   ☐ ☐ ☐ ☐ ☐
38. Administrators in my school adjust priorities to support professional risk taking and experimentation.   ☐ ☐ ☐ ☐ ☐

6

School Culture Survey page 2.

Correspondence From Kenneth Leithwood

The internal reliabilities of each of the surveys are reported in Figure 10.1 of page 110 in the edition you purchased. Of course these reliabilities change marginally depending on the data set being used. But what is reported here is pretty representative of what we have found across many administrations.

The validity question is a bit more complicated. But I point to the research evidence on which the constructs and items are based as the main source of validity. What this means is that the items and constructs directly reflect the best evidence that was available when they were constructed about components of the school and district that explain variation in achievement and mediating organizational quality.

smithboy@email.uophx.edu writes:
>Professor Leithwood
>My name is Andrew Smith and I am the principal of an elementary school in
>Yuma County, AZ working toward the Doctor of Management degree at the
>University of Phoenix in Phoenix, AZ. I recently purchased your book
>Making Schools Smarter, 2nd edition. I am interested in using the school
>culture survey (p. 136-137) in the book for my research. I am correlating
>the relationship between school culture and standardized test scores
>(Stanford-9) for my dissertation.
>
>First, I would like to know the validity and reliability of that survey.
>Second, may I have permission (in writing) to use the survey as a
>research instrument. I have found your book very useful as culture and
>relationships are the focus of our school district at this time. I called
>Corwin Press about the validity and reliability and they informed me that
>they would be contacting the editor or author of the book. However, I was
>researching on the net and your name came up at the University of Toronto
>so I decided to email you.
>
>Thank you and I appreciate your valuable time and consideration.
>
>p.s. I can send you a receipt of my purchase of your book if that is
>necessary. I purchased it through Amazon

APPENDIX E: DEMOGRAPHIC SURVEY

Demographic Information (no names please)

Name of school (names not used in final edit of study)_____

Gender (circle)   M   F

Age   _____25-29 _____30-34 _____40-44 _____45-49 _____50-54 _____55+

   Years of experience in teaching (total)   _____

   Years of experience as an administrator (total)   _____

   Years of experience at 2003-2004 school   _____

   Grade taught during 2003-2004   _____

   Race (circle)   White   Black   Hispanic   Asian   Other

APPENDIX F: CORRESPONDENCE REGARDING THE STANFORD

ACHIEVEMENT TEST, NINTH EDITION

Correspondence regarding the use of the Stanford Achievement Test: Ninth

Edition from Harcourt Assessment, Inc. This letter is from the Legal Affairs Office.

Dear Mr. Smith:

Thank you for your e-mail correspondence regarding the use of the data from
the Stanford Achievement Test: Ninth Edition in your dissertation.
Because you state you are not using actual items or sample items from the
test materials and because all the resulting data from testing is owned by
the Arizona Department of Education there is no need for us to grant you
permission to use the data. Any permission needed for the use of the data
should be obtained from the Arizona Department of Education.

Thank you for your interest in our products.

Sincerely,

Robin Snyder
Contract Specialist
Legal Affairs
Harcourt Assessment, Inc.
19500 Bulverde Road
San Antonio, TX 78259
Robin_Snyder@Harcourt.com

"Andrew L. Smith"
To: <Robin_Snyder@Harcourt.com>
Subject: Use of Stanfod-9 in a dissertation
05/25/2004 08:53 AM

Dear Ms. Snyder,

In February I wrote to you regarding the usage of the Stanford Achievement
Test: Ninth Edition in my dissertation. You responded regarding the
parameters, and I appreciated your quick response. However, I telephoned to
let you know that I am not using the test, but just the results from the
test via the Arizona Department of Education. You mentioned that no

permission was necessary because the actually test is not being used, but rather the results. I am asking if you could state that to me (that permission is not necessary to use the results) via email for my records. Thank you again for all of your time and information.
Andy

Andrew L. Smith
smithboy@email.uophx.edu
[Address]
[Phone number]

APPENDIX G: YUMA COUNTY PROFILE

Permission to use the Yuma County, Arizona profile produced by the Arizona

Department of Commerce.

Andrew: Thank you for your request - it is certainly granted.

Best wishes to you,

Alisa Lyons
Arizona Department of Commerce
alisal@azcommerce.com
Our Job is JOBS!
-----Original Message-----
From: Andrew L. Smith [mailto:smithboy@email.uophx.edu]
Sent: Friday, June 11, 2004 9:26 AM
To: alisal@azcommerce.com
Subject: Use of Yuma County Profile

    Alisa,
    I am writing to obtain permission to use the Yuma County, Arizona
    profile produced by the Arizona Department of Commerce. I am currently a
    Doctor of Management student at the University of Phoenix, Phoenix, AZ.
    My dissertation research regards school organizational culture and
    student achievement throughout Yuma County. I wish to use the profile as
    it will help the reader understand the economic dimensions of the county
    with regard to population, employment, and geographic land distribution,
    and income. Upon completion the dissertation will be published.

    Thank you for your help and time, it is appreciated.
    Andy

    Andrew L. Smith
    [e-mail address]
    [Address]
    [Phone number]

Profile:

Yuma County, Arizona

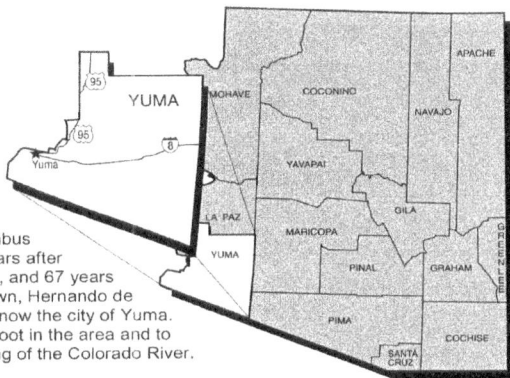

Yuma County was one of the original four counties designated by the First Territorial Legislature. Until 1983, when voters decided to split it into La Paz County in the north and a new Yuma County in the south, it maintained its original boundaries.

In 1540, just 48 years after Columbus discovered the New World, 18 years after the conquest of Mexico by Cortéz, and 67 years before the settlement of Jamestown, Hernando de Alarcón visited the site of what is now the city of Yuma. He was the first European to set foot in the area and to recognize the best natural crossing of the Colorado River.

From the 1850s through the 1870s, steamboats on the Colorado River transported passengers and goods to mines, ranches and military outposts in the area, serving the ports of Yuma, Laguna, Castle Dome, Norton's Landing, Ehrenberg, Aubry, Ft. Mohave and Hardyville.

For many years, Yuma served as the gateway to the new western territory of California. In 1870, the Southern Pacific Railroad bridged the river, and Yuma became a hub for the railroad and was selected as the county seat.

Much of Yuma County's 5,519 square miles is desert land accented by rugged mountains. The valley regions, however, contain an abundance of arable land, which is irrigated with Colorado River water. Agriculture, tourism, military and government are the county's principal industries. During the winter months, the population grows considerably with part-time residents. All of Yuma County is an Enterprise Zone.

The U.S. Bureau of Land Management accounts for 42 percent of land ownership; Indian reservations, less than 0.5 percent; the state of Arizona, 5 percent; individual or corporate, 13 percent; and other public lands, 40 percent.

ARIZONA DEPARTMENT OF COMMERCE
Our Job is JOBS!

1700 W. Washington Street, Phoenix, Arizona 85007 (602) 771-1100
www.azcommerce.com

137

Yuma County
At-A-Glance

County Seat:	Yuma
2004 Population:	181,470
2004 Labor Force:	75,982
Unemployment Rate:	23.5%
Major Industries:	Agriculture, Military, Retail Trade Tourism
Best Paying Industries:	Agriculture, Government, Manufacturing, Transportation/ Public Utilities

Sources: Population Estimates July 2004, Population Statistics Unit, Research Administration Arizona Department of Economic Security; December 2004 Special Unemployment Report, Arizona Department of Economic Security, Research Administration.

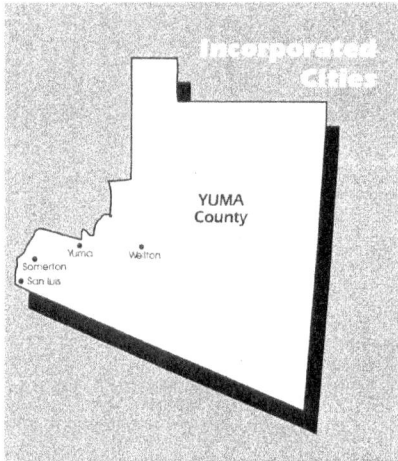

YUMA County

Somerton
Yuma
Wellton
San Luis

Population

	1990	2000	2004
Arizona	3,665,228	5,130,632	5,833,685
Yuma County	106,895	160,026	181,470

Major Cities/Communities

Cocopah Indian Reservation	515	1,025	N/A
San Luis	4,212	15,322	21,180
Somerton	5,282	7,266	8,855
Wellton	1,066	1,829	1,900
Yuma	54,923	77,515	86,070

Source: U.S. Census Bureau and Arizona Department of Economic Security, Population Statistics Unit
N/A - Not available

Age Distribution

	% of total
0-14	24.40%
15-24	14.55%
25-44	25.62%
45-64	18.91%
65+	16.53%

Source: U.S. Census Bureau, April 1, 2000 Census

Population Composition*

Race	% of total
White	68.3%
African American	2.2%
Native American	1.6%
Asian or Pacific Islander	1.0%
Other	26.8%
Totals	100.0%
Hispanic Heritage*	50.5%

Source: U.S. Census Bureau, April 1, 2000 Census
* Persons of Hispanic heritage may be of any race

2004 Civilian Labor Force

	Labor Force	Unemployment Rate
Arizona	2,762,612	4.8%
Yuma County	75,982	22.9%
Major Cities/Communities		
Cocopah Indian Reservation	290	15.9%
San Luis	4,242	64.5%
Somerton	3,371	42.3%
Wellton	689	22.2%
Yuma	40,607	15.8%

Source: Arizona Dept. of Economic Security, December 2004 Special Unemployment Report

Labor Force

2004 Employment by Sector

Mining & Construction	4,400
Education & Health Srvs	5,900
Financial Activities	1,400
Government	13,700
Information	1,100
Leisure & Hospitality	4,900
Manufacturing	2,900
Professional & Business Srvs	3,300
Trade, Transportation & Utilities	9,700

Source: Prepared in cooperation with the U.S. Department of Labor, Bureau of Labor
Statistics, State of Arizona Economic Security Research Administration.
Figures are organized under the North American Industrial Classification System (NAICS).

2004 Total All Occupations

Employment	56,010
Hourly Compensation	
Median Wage	$10.21
Average Wage	$13.08
Entry Wage	$ 6.04
Experienced	$15.96

2004 Employment by Occupation - Average Wages

	Employment	Avg Wages
Farming, Fishing & Forestry	7,570	$ 7.62
Office & Administrative Support	8,120	$11.79
Transportation & Material Moving	5,510	$10.29
Sales & Related Occupations	4,650	$12.35
Food Preparation & Serving Related	4,430	$ 7.66
Education, Training & Library	3,500	$14.65
Construction & Extraction	3,910	$13.05
Management	1,860	$30.54

Source: Prepared by the Ariz. Dept. of Economic Security, Research Administration in
cooperation with the U.S. Department of Labor, Bureau of Labor Statistics, June 2005

Major Employers

Employer	Employment Type
Alexander Automotive	New and Used Car Dealer
Arizona Public Service	Public Utilities
Arizona State Government	Government
Arizona Western College	Education
Barkley Farms	Cash Grains
Bravo Packing Co.	Crop Service
Cocopah Bingo Casino	Misc. Recreation Services
Cocopah Indian Tribe	Government
Crane School District #13	Education
Direct Marketing	Call Center
Dole Corporation	Fruits and Vegetables
Emco Harvesting Co.	Farm Labor and Management
Factor Sales, San Luis	Retail
Gilpin's Construction	General Contractors
	Steel Fabrication Shop
Gowan Company	Agricultural Chemical
Grower's Company, Inc.	Crop Service
Home Depot	Retail
J.C. Penney Company	Department Store
Life Care Center of Yuma	Nursing
Lowe's	Retail
Marine Corps Air Station (MCAS)	Government
Marlin Packing, Inc.	Citrus Grower and Packer
McElhaney Cattle Company	Livestock
Mission Citrus	Crop Services
Palmview Rehabilitation & Care Center	Nursing
Pasquinelli Produce Co.	Fruits and Vegetables
RMH Teleservices, Inc.	Call Center
Russell	Commercial Refrigeration
Salyer American Fresh Foods	Produce Cooler and Shipper
Sam's Club	Retail
Sears	Department Stores
Shay Oil Co.	Retail Gasoline & Sales
Sky View Cooling	Produce Grower, Cooler and Shipper
Southern Pacific Transportation Co.	Railroads
Spherion	Call Center
Super K-Mart	Department Store
Shaw Industries/Queen Carpet	Manufacturer/Carpet Yarn Carpet Corp.
Target	Retail
Tillman	Protective Clothing manufacturer
U.S. Army Proving Ground	Government
U.S. Border Patrol	Immigration
U.S. Department of Interior Bureau of Reclamation	Government
U.S. Postal Service	Government
Wal Mart	Department Store
Western Arizona Council of Governments	Social Services
Western Newspaper	Newspaper publisher
The Sun	Newspaper publisher
Weyerhaeuser Co.	Manufacturer/Corrugated Boxes
Yuma City Government	Government
Yuma County Government	Government
Yuma Elementary School District	Government
Yuma Regional Medical Center	General Medical Surgical Hospital

Source: Local sources

Utilities

Electric Service

Major Supplier:

APS	(800) 253-9407
Wellton-Mohawk Irrigation & Drainage Irrigation & Power District	(928) 785-3351

Natural Gas Service

Major Supplier:

Southwest Gas Corporation	(800) 766-9722

Water and Sewer

Check individual community profile for water and sewer available locally or call individual town for more information.

Telephone

Major Suppliers:

Qwest	(800) 244-1111

Medical

Yuma Regional Medical Center, Yuma   (928) 344-2000

Education

Arizona Western College, Yuma	(928) 344-7656
Southern Illinois University, Yuma	(928) 726-7170
University of Phoenix, Yuma	(928) 341-0233
Northern Arizona University, Yuma	(928) 317-6402

Transportation

Highways

Interstate 8, U.S. 95, Highway 80

Bus Lines

Greyhound Bus Lines   (800) 231-2222

Rail Service

Union Pacific Railroad	(888) 870-8777
Yuma Valley Railway Tourist Railroad	(928) 783-3456

Trucking Service

Con-Way Western Express, Central Freight Lines, Consolidated Freightways, Gale Transfer, LA Yuma Freight Lines Inc., Pacific Scales, Roadway Express, San Luis International Freight Service, Yellow Freight Systems Inc.

Air Service

Major Airport

Airport Name:
    Yuma International   (928) 726-5882
    2191 E. 32nd St.
    Functional Class: Commercial Service
    Elevation: 213'
    Ownership: Public/Yuma County
    Use: Public/Commercial/Military
    Served by: United Express/Yuma - LAX
    America West Express/Yuma - PHX
    Nav-Aids: ILS/PAR
    Runway: 3L/21R   Length: 13,300'   Width: 200'
    Surface: Concrete
    Runway: 3R/21L   Length: 9,239'   Width: 150'
    Surface: Asphalt, concrete
    Runway: 08/26   Length: 6,145'   Width: 150'
    Surface: Asphalt, Concrete
    General Purpose Foreign Trade: Zone #219

Source   Department of Transportation, Arizona Airports Land Use Compatibility Study

Distance to Major Cities

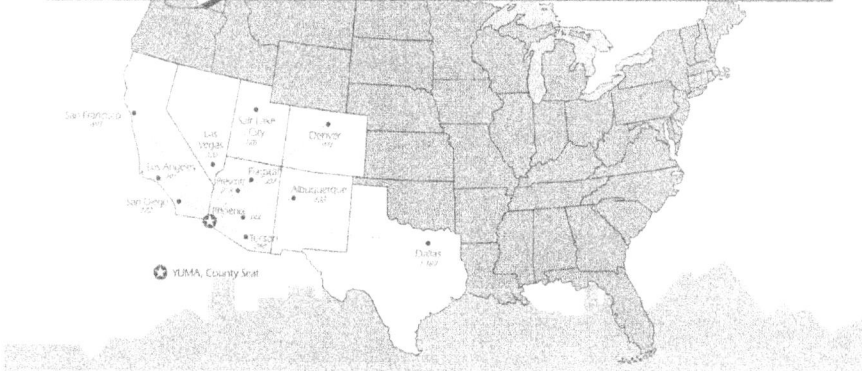